"I've always been grateful for Jeff Vanderstelt's heart for discipleship. Rather than drawing people to himself, he labors to help others understand the power they possess in the Spirit. He does what all good leaders should do: spends his days equipping others to do the work of the ministry."

Francis Chan, *New York Times* best-selling author, *Crazy Love* and *Forgotten God*

"*Saturate* is a compelling and biblically serious picture of Jesus and the mission he has given his people. It is a book that is deeply doctrinal and helpfully applicable. I have known Jeff to faithfully live out the philosophies of life and day-to-day ministry contained in these pages, and have watched firsthand as God produced much fruit. I pray it encourages you."

Matt Chandler, Lead Pastor, The Village Church, Dallas, Texas; President, Acts 29 Church Planting Network

"Jeff is one of the smartest, most dedicated, and most interesting disciplemakers I know. In this book, and through the medium of his life story, he effectively passes on the key insights that make him one of the best movement leaders in the country. *Saturate* is a winner."

Alan Hirsch, Founder, Forge and Future Travelers; award-winning author, *Untamed*, *Right Here Right Now*, and *ReJesus*

"If someone were to ask me where to go to learn about discipleship, I would hand them the Bible along with Jeff Vanderstelt's book *Saturate*. Readers will find themselves taking a survey of their lives, seeing the areas that God desires to take captive for his glory. Whether you are a preacher, homemaker, small-group leader, high school student, or new convert, *Saturate* will spur you on to live a life that will influence others to know Jesus while growing people in Jesus, not just at church, but in all of life."

Jackie Hill-Perry, poet; writer; hip-hop artist

"This is a thought-provoking, heart-warming account of a body of believers taking God's call to live as family seriously. Don't allow yourself to be distracted by the details or to quibble with the incidentals. This book challenges and encourages all of us to intentionally live on mission in the mundane details and events of everyday life."

Steve Timmis, Executive Director, Acts 29 Church Planting Network

"Jeff Vanderstelt uses an ordinary experience to give us extraordinary insight into what it means to be a disciple of Jesus. *Saturate* is a great challenge to all of us to stop doing church and be the church!"

Dave Ferguson, Lead Pastor, Community Christian Church, Naperville, Illinois; Lead Visionary, NewThing

"In *Saturate*, Jeff Vanderstelt endeavors to provide Christians with an image of God's grace that is all-encompassing and inescapable. Whether you are new to the faith or a seasoned believer, Jeff's words will encourage you and focus God's gospel on every facet of your life. This book will challenge the way you see your Savior, your mission, and your everyday life."

Ed Stetzer, President, LifeWay Research; author, *Subversive Kingdom*; www.edstetzer.com

"Jeff Vanderstelt's passion and commitment to the fame of Jesus are as evident in this book as they are in his preaching. It was so refreshing to read chapter after chapter that lifted high the name of Jesus and to be challenged to do the same more and more in my life and ministry."

Matt Carter, Pastor of Preaching, The Austin Stone Community Church, Austin, Texas; co-author, *The Real Win*

"*Saturate* is a crucially needed and down-to-earth manual for what is most important—loving God and loving neighbors. What Christian wouldn't want to know what Jeff Vanderstelt has brilliantly and helpfully given us here?"

Jared C. Wilson, Director of Content Strategy, Midwestern Baptist Theological Seminary; author, *Gospel Wakefulness* and *The Prodigal Church*

SATURATE

SATURATE

Being Disciples of Jesus
in the Everyday Stuff of Life

JEFF VANDERSTELT

WHEATON, ILLINOIS

Saturate: Being Disciples of Jesus in the Everyday Stuff of Life

Copyright © 2015 by Jeff Vanderstelt

Published by Crossway
        1300 Crescent Street
        Wheaton, Illinois 60187

Published in association with Yates & Yates, www.yates2.com

Cover design: Erik Maldre

Interior illustrations: James Graves, Visual Jams

First printing 2015

Printed in the United States of America

Hardcover ISBN: 978-1-4335-4599-3
ePub ISBN: 978-1-4335-4602-0
PDF ISBN: 978-1-4335-4600-6
Mobipocket ISBN: 978-1-4335-4601-3

Library of Congress Cataloging-in-Publication Data
Vanderstelt, Jeff, 1969–
Saturate : being disciples of Jesus in the everyday stuff
of life / Jeff Vanderstelt.
    pages cm
  Includes bibliographical references and index.
  ISBN 978-1-4335-4599-3 (hc)
1. Christian life. I. Title.
BV4501.3.V365   2015
248.4—dc23   2014036805

Crossway is a publishing ministry of Good News Publishers.

LB		26	25	24	23	22	21	20	19	18	17
14	13	12	11	10	9	8	7	6	5	4	3

To

The Soma Tacoma family.
Thank you for ten great years!
"You are our glory and joy"
(1 Thess. 2:20).

Mom and Dad.
God used you to plant the seeds.
Saturate is part of your legacy.

Jayne, Haylee, Caleb, and Maggie.
You are my greatest gifts.
You all bring me great joy!

Nicki.
This book is written in your memory.
Distant neighbor who became sister, mother, grandmother,
and friend,
you are finally with the man of your dreams!

Contents

Acknowledgments

This book exists because of the prodding of many people. I certainly prefer speaking over writing, but the elders from Soma Tacoma, along with several leaders from churches that belong to the Soma family, urged me to write. They were relentless. I owe them a great deal of gratitude, both for pushing me forward and for giving me the space to dedicate time to this work.

I also am indebted to the Soma Tacoma family. We have struggled together, failed forward, and grown in grace, and we have more stories of God's faithfulness to tell than there are pages in this book. I am so thankful to God for each man, woman, and child who has been part of the body of Christ on mission together in Tacoma these past ten years. This book represents our learning together. It has been a joy to grow with these dear brothers and sisters.

I am also grateful to my assistant, Sara Parker, who served me so well. Without her help, this book would not have been completed. Randy and Lisa Sheets' encouragement kept me from throwing in the towel; they constantly reassured me that what is written on these pages will serve people well. And the Wedge missional community, every iteration of it for the past ten years, has its fingerprints all over this book. Life together has been beautifully redemptive.

Lastly, Jayne, my truth-telling, Jesus-loving, Spirit-filled, praying wife, has kept me grounded, keeps it real, and prods us all to keep looking heavenward with faith-drenched, hope-filled expectancy that our Father has great plans in store for us all. God knew I needed a partner and friend like Jayne. Not only would I not have written a book, I wouldn't have the ministry I have without her.

Introduction

I don't like to write.

In fact, I have avoided writing a book for more than six years. But I couldn't hold back any longer, because my heart has been captured by a vision that I cannot shake.

This vision is Jesus saturation—every man, woman, and child in every place having a daily encounter with Jesus through words spoken and deeds done through his people.

This isn't really my vision. It is God's vision. He says, "For the earth will be filled with the knowledge of the glory of the LORD as the waters cover the sea" (Hab. 2:14). And God will accomplish this vision through his Son, Jesus Christ, working through his body, the church. Ephesians 1:22–23 says, "He put all things under his feet and gave him as head over all things to the church, which is his body, the fullness of him who fills all in all."

Jesus is the head of his body, the church, through which he intends to fill every place with his presence. This is saturation—Jesus saturation.

Can you imagine every city, every neighborhood, every street, and every house saturated with Jesus's presence through his people? What if, in every school, every classroom, and every extracurricular activity, students daily experienced the person and work of Jesus? Can you dream with me of a day when no business office, retail center, or industrial hub can get away from the good news of Jesus proclaimed in words and expressed in gracious deeds? A day when every café, pub, restaurant, or bakery smells of the aroma of Christ?

This is God's intention for his world. And his plan is to do it through his people.

He wants you to be a part of it!

I hope you are reading this book because you want to be part of this. If you know, trust, love, and follow Jesus, you are part of it. If you haven't yet submitted your life to Jesus, I pray you will. Jesus saturation can't happen *through* you until it's happened *to* you.

As you read these pages, you, like others, may think this book and its message are for the spiritual elite: a special group of Christians who are uniquely called of God, the paid staff members of a church, or the professionally trained. Don't believe that lie. It isn't true.

Or maybe you think the only people through whom God works are the radicals who sell all they have and go into foreign lands. He certainly works through them. But he also works through people who stay. His plan is to work through all of us in every place.

It's possible that you've never experienced Jesus working through you to fill every place you go with his presence. Don't let that prevent you from believing he wants to and is able to. The truth is, if you belong to Jesus, you are called to participate in his vision of saturation.

To be clear, this is not a leadership book, though I hope leaders will read it and benefit from it. Rather, this book is written to encourage the everyday Jesus follower to engage in the everyday stuff of life with the goal of seeing Jesus saturation for everyone in every place.

This book is for you—the normal, unimpressive, everyday person, young or old, male or female—because Jesus means to carry out his mission of filling the world with his presence through you. You are *meant* to do this.

The mission of Jesus is yours to participate in. It has always been God's intention to choose normal, everyday people, and to show his amazing power and glory through them. He's not looking for the most impressive person because he already is that person.

You are a perfect candidate for God to use to accomplish his purpose!

The people you will read about in this book are perfect candidates too. They are real, everyday, normal, unimpressive people. (Well, *I'm* impressed with them because I know them, love them, and have seen Jesus do remarkable things in and through their lives.) They are no different from you. What is most impressive about them is not they themselves, but Jesus at work in and through them. That is what Jesus saturation is really about—him filling us so he can fill the world through us.

I pray your journey through the following pages will lead you to become a disciple of Jesus on his mission in the everyday stuff of life and will result in exceedingly great joy for you as Jesus works through you to fill the world with his glory for his fame. What greater purpose and joy could there be?

I don't know your starting point on this journey, but let's begin where Jesus woke me up to this vision. It began in a boat.

Part 1

Beginnings

(1)

It Began in a Boat

The sun was shimmering off the smooth water of Hamlin Lake. The lines on our poles hung quietly undisturbed in the water. We hadn't had a bite for a while.

I enjoyed these moments with my dad. Though I loved catching fish, I was also fine just looking at the water and being with my father. And I needed some time for nothing: no sound, no conversation, no work. Just space.

I had been a youth pastor for twelve years, but was at a crossroad. I had served in three churches and had experienced what many would call success in all of them. However, it was clear to everyone around me that I no longer fit the youth pastor role.

I was the director of Student Impact, the high school ministry at Willow Creek Community Church in South Barrington, Illinois. I had started off strong there as we restructured the ministry to better mobilize the students for mission to their campuses. At the beginning, it seemed as if I was the golden boy. People loved me. The team followed my lead. The ministry grew considerably. The leadership above me seemed to believe in me. I had taken on a position that needed a catalytic thinker with a new vision and strategy, and I had delivered. But eventually I had found myself in a management position, with a team that was losing trust in me. I didn't fit any longer. I had gotten into ministry because I loved seeing people's lives changed, and I had gone into youth ministry because teenagers, in their youthful idealism, believe they can be a significant part of changing the world. Now I was largely running an organization and becoming more and more distant from people.

As a result, I had fallen into a deep depression and had started seeing a counselor. I was anxious, afraid, and felt like a failure. Most nights, I tossed and turned till dawn, barely able to sleep. My wife, Jayne, had to regularly wash the bed sheets because they were drenched with my anxious sweat. I pondered the purpose of my life and how I could continue in the work I had in front of me. My heart agonized over what to do next. Some nights, I contemplated suicide. We had a newborn daughter and a newly purchased house, but I was clueless about our future. I knew I needed to get away from it all for a few days.

I needed God to speak.

I needed direction.

I needed help.

And I needed to be with my dad on the lake.

"Clearly Something Is Broken"

For some time, we didn't speak. I like that about fishing—I don't have to talk. I needed that quietness.

Finally, Dad broke the silence: "Did you know we just hired a discipleship pastor at our church? Your mother and I really like him. He's been training us to be disciples of Jesus who make disciples. We've been in the church for over fifty years now, but we've never been trained to do that. We've been having these neighborhood parties and getting into discussions about Jesus. Your mother and I are learning a lot and really enjoying it."

My dad continued to share that when his church hired its new discipleship pastor, the majority of the members didn't know how to obey Jesus's command to make disciples. Now, they were seeing that it should be normal for everyone to do it.

As he spoke, I thought of all the years I had worked with youth. I'll never forget the first student I led to faith in Jesus—Lynn. As soon as she believed, her adoptive parents kicked her out of the house. The families in our church took her into their homes and treated her as if she was one of them while she struggled forward in her faith. Her life was messy, but in the mess, she brought many others to join our community of faith.

I pictured many afternoons going through Bible stories after school with Pedro, a freshman, and his friends Jessica, Jennifer, and Adam. I laughed thinking about Jessica, who had no Bible knowledge at all, saying Joseph's new name over and over again—"Zaphenath-paneah, Zaphenath-paneah, Zaphenath-paneah"—because it sounded funny to her.

I remembered Todd, whom I walked with from seventh grade through high school. He was a shy kid whose passion came out on the field of sports. He hardly spoke out about Jesus at first, but eventually he grew to disciple boys younger than him. I thought of Nick, who, as a junior, was the life of the party. God grabbed hold of his life, transformed him, and used him to lead dozens of his classmates to Jesus—in the halls, at parties, or at a restaurant after a football game.

One of those classmates was Stephan. He had a very sad story. His mother had left him on the side of the road when he was a little boy. Eventually, he found his way through the foster system and landed in a boys' home. Stephan came to believe he had a loving Father in God because of Jesus. He went from being a lost orphan to becoming one of God's children.

Name after name, face after face, kept coming to my mind. All of these kids were everyday teenagers whom Jesus had worked in and through to accomplish great stuff.

All of them had become disciple makers.

In other words, all of them could tell the story of God's love for them through Jesus. All were growing in knowing, believing, and obeying the Scriptures. They prayed for people regularly and saw many friends come to follow, obey, and depend on Jesus as well.

Some did it through sports, others in the classroom, and many just by hanging out together and talking about Jesus in normal life. They loved being together and were excited about Jesus, and that excitement spilled out into everyone around them.

As I thought of all these kids and what my dad had just said, I found myself angry and dumbfounded. "How is it possible that someone could be in the church for over fifty years and not know how to make disciples?" I wondered. "What's wrong with the church? I've witnessed teens begin to do this in a matter of months. And why would you hire a discipleship pastor when the whole point of the church is making disciples of Jesus? It's not a separate program of the church! It's the mission of the whole church! Every disciple of Jesus is called to it.

"Clearly something is broken!"

You Are the Church

My dad continued to talk about the training he and my mom were receiving. He spoke about the parties they were throwing, the neighbors who were attending, and the conversations they were having. I was excited for his newfound ministry, but I was also sad, because as I thought about what it was like growing up in our house, I realized my parents had been doing much of this for years.

My parents were the epitome of hospitality. They arranged their lives and home so that people would want to be there. It didn't seem remarkable to me when I was growing up; it was all I knew. They put a pool in the backyard. My dad remodeled our basement and set up a pool table, Ping Pong table, coin-operated video games, and pinball machines. Our house was the place for teenagers to party because the door was always open and my mom always had the pantry fully stocked with food and drink. It was clear my parents wanted people there. It was completely normal to come home from a night out with my friends to find my parents hanging out with a group of teenagers. I'd walk in and hear them having a conversation about sports, school, dating, sex—you name it.

It seemed a little weird when I thought about it: "Why would teenagers want to hang out with my parents and talk about sex?" I wondered. "What do my parents know about sex?"

It also was not unusual during dinner for my parents to bring up a person who was in need of a place to stay: a boy whose parents had kicked him out of the house; a husband who was not doing well in his marriage and needed a break; or an ex-drug addict who needed shelter from peers who wanted to pull him back into the world of narcotics. There were dozens of these stories over the years. After they would share such a story, my parents would ask us four boys: "Should we invite him to live with us? Would one of you like to give up your room for a while?" I can't say that was always easy for us. What teenage boy wants to give up his bedroom to a stranger? However, there are many men today who call Jesus their Lord and the Vanderstelts their family because of the way my mom and dad included them.

"If my parents didn't know how to make disciples, what were they doing all those years?" I asked myself.

As I stared at the water, it dawned on me that no one had ever validated what my mom and dad did. It didn't fit into the mold of church programs. The leadership of the church never told them that they were doing the work of the church in their home. Church had been wrongly defined *only* as an event: a Bible study on Wednesday or a class and the worship service on Sunday.

People *went* to church. It was an event or a program. Church wasn't seen as the people of God doing the work of God in everyday life. What my parents did, didn't count—or at least that's what they believed.

That day in the boat was a defining moment in my life. As I look back, I recognize that the Spirit of God was showing me a deficiency in how the church was understood and structured and how discipleship was defined and practiced.

The reason the teenagers I worked with were able to make disciples of Jesus was that they believed they *were* the church. For them, church wasn't something you *go to*. Church was something *you are*.

This is confusing to some because the word *church* literally means "gathering." So people naturally think it is something you go to—after all, you go to a gathering.

However, when the Bible uses the word *church*, it is referring to God's people gathered to Jesus to do his work in the world. The teens were the *Jesus-gathered people* sent to the soccer team, the classroom, and the party on Friday night, to do Jesus's work of loving others toward him. My parents were no different. Neither were those who surrounded Jesus.

Neither are you.

When you read the accounts of Jesus's life in the Bible, you see this. You discover the everyday, messed-up people that Jesus gathered around himself to do his work. You see warriors and women, fishermen and fathers, pagans and prostitutes, the religious and the ragamuffins. And you see Jesus in the middle of all of them, doing the work of God with them in the marketplace, at a party, on a mountainside, in a house—and on a fishing boat on a calm lake where there seemed to be no fish.

He still does his work on quiet fishing boats in the middle of calm waters far away from religious gatherings. He was doing it in me, right there with my dad.

Everyday People Doing Everyday Stuff

It was then that I realized something. The youth I had worked with had experienced something closer to church than my parents' generation had. These kids were the simple, regular, messed-up people that Jesus had chosen to use in everyday life.

My parents weren't alone.

I was one of them as well.

I began to realize that I didn't fit the typical mold of a church leader either. Yes, I could preach on a stage, but I didn't fit the "church-as-event-only" approach anymore. I wanted to see people, all people, all kinds of people in every place, mobilized to be the "Jesus-gathered people" on his mission.

Then I started to think about all the youth I had worked with over the years and considered where they were. It occurred to me that many had come to believe the same thing my parents had. They didn't see themselves as a key part of the church anymore. What they did didn't seem to count. They had graduated into what the kids called "big church." They had gone from actively seeking to reach their peers through the everyday stuff of life to being asked to sit in the bleachers and watch someone else play the game. They had joined the thousands of people who unwittingly believe the lie that church is only an event you attend and that the mission of God is accomplished on a stage where only a few do the ministry in front of the many.

As a teenager, I played goalie on a hockey team that traveled throughout Michigan. At one point, I had the opportunity to step up into a higher division, a change that could have led to a hockey career. However, our family had friends who had played professional hockey, and hearing from them about the lifestyle on the road toward a hockey career made it unappealing to me. Besides, at that point in my life, I was planning to become a lawyer. So I turned down the opportunity, and with that, I stopped playing hockey altogether. I hung up my skates. In fact, I even stopped watching the game. It was a sad moment—a kind of death moment for me. I died to being a hockey player. I figured, "Why keep playing when there is nowhere to go from here but down?" I didn't want a regular reminder that I could have done more but chose not to.

This is what had happened to many of the teenagers I had led. Some of them had just taken their seats. They gave, they attended, they invited, and they served from time to time. But they were sitting most of the time. Some of them had become disillusioned with the church. They had been key players in the game. They had experienced the victories, but they had been demoted to being spectators! I think they figured that if all they were ever going to do was just watch after having played the game, then why should they even be around the game at all? Some had left the church altogether, I'm sad to say. Others had found themselves involved in college campus ministries or overseas work—places that still believed everyone should be in the game—while others had gone on to join new expressions of the church that were calling them back into the game of everyday mission. In many cases, the local churches lost some of their best players.

There I was, in a boat with my dad—and with Jesus. My

dad didn't see it, but Jesus had been with him all along—and with me. He had been in all of those acts of love, open doors, and late-evening conversations. Jesus had been in the midst of his church, doing his work through my parents' lives. My mom and dad didn't need to be trained in a new form of discipleship. They needed to know that all those years they had been creating opportunities for disciples of Jesus to be made. They just needed to be equipped in how to engage those opportunities more intentionally with Jesus.

Several times throughout the next couple of days, I shared with my parents how they should see what they had always done as the ministry of the church—they could make disciples of Jesus in their home. A spark was ignited in their hearts and they began to get excited about how God had uniquely designed them for his purposes in the world. What they did mattered! He could use them as they were.

And even though they didn't know it, they had been discipling their own children while they were reaching out to others, so their example had deeply shaped me.

A New Beginning

Months passed after that time on the water, but the thoughts I'd had that day didn't leave me. "Something has to be done about this!" I kept thinking. I believed there was a need to call normal people to see all of life as the context for Jesus's ministry to happen. Everyone could be and should be a part of this. And the everyday stuff of life matters—Jesus wants to see his church engage in all of life for his purposes.

When I finally resigned from my position four months later, I believed I would never serve in a vocational capacity in any church again. The leadership had graciously paid for me to receive a thorough assessment, which revealed that I should be involved in new business start-ups, consulting, or catalytic leadership. The assessors warned me against ever getting into a management position again and clearly directed me away from church leadership unless it was church planting.

At that point, I really didn't think the church had a place for someone like me. I thought: "Why not fall back on your business degree and start a company? Make disciples of Jesus as a businessman and then teach others to do the same. Maybe you could be an encouragement to businessmen like Dad, who were never told business could be done as ministry." I also wondered: "How can Jayne and I partner together for ministry in and around our home? What if we could retrain people to see that the mission of the church can be done in the home and the marketplace?"

The day I stepped down, I received three phone calls, all from people unaware that I had resigned. Each call was an invitation to be a church planter. One of them was from a former mentor of mine. He invited me back to the greater Seattle area to plant churches with him. As he described what he felt called to do and invited me into it, I sensed a nudge from the Holy Spirit: "This is the beginning of what I started to birth in your heart on the boat. I'm in this. Trust me as I lead you into something new."

Not fully grasping what we were embarking on, Jayne, Haylee (our ten-month-old daughter), and I found ourselves, two months later, in January 2003, driving across the country in our minivan, ready to use our life savings to support us as we began planting churches where everyone is involved in the work and every part of life counts—where people like my mom and dad, single moms, teenage boys, and fisherman have a part to play.

2

Jesus Goes to
Poker Parties

"I'll raise you a hundred," Greg said as he pushed a stack of poker chips into the middle of the table to show he meant business. At the same time, laughter erupted from the next room, where the ladies were sharing stories about marriage and motherhood. Greg's wife, Mary, listened as the women poured out their hearts to one another.

This was the first time Greg and Mary had been at our house for one of our parties.[1] Jayne and I had been in the Puget Sound area for about a year, and we were beginning to call people together to *be* the church in the greater Tacoma area. Parties and feasts were one of the means we were using to gather people

---

[1] This poker game was primarily a recreational activity. I do not promote gambling, as I am very aware that many people have experienced addictive and destructive results.

and give them a taste of what it might look like to be the church in our community.

In the past, several of us in the Chicago suburbs had experienced community forming this way around meals and celebrations. Caesar and Tina had introduced us to the art of hospitality and the joy of the party. Tina is an amazing cook, and she and Caesar hosted the best dinner parties around. If they were hosting a dinner, you did not want to miss it!

At one of these dinners, about three courses into an amazing five-course meal, it dawned on us: "This is a great picture of the kingdom of God!" While immersed in the feast of food and life together, we recalled Jesus comparing the kingdom of God to a feast where everyone is invited in (Luke 14:12–24). Together we started to imagine what the church would be like if we all believed we were a picture of God's kingdom breaking into the world in ways that felt like a party. One of us said: "If the church believed this, it would radically change what we do and how we live! We would be known as the most celebratory people around. Word would spread. People who wouldn't normally want to come to a church event would come to our homes. Who wouldn't want to be a part of that?"

A seed was planted in our hearts at that moment, and the conversation never really ended. We began to ask questions: What if we were to start a church that feasted and celebrated around Jesus together? What if our homes were intended by God to be some of the primary spaces in which the ministry of the church should take place? People could be welcomed in, cared for, and experience belonging to a people who enjoy one another and life together. This would transform people's perceptions of the church. Their understanding of who the church is and what she does would be very different from others'. As a result, people would come to understand Jesus in an entirely new way. If church were more like a feast and ministry took place regularly in our homes, everyone could join and anyone could do it. Everyone loves to feast and celebrate together, and anyone who knows and loves Jesus can host a party around him.

Jesus's church celebrates and feasts together. His people live life to the fullest for his glory and learn how to do the normal, everyday stuff of life for his glory. Not just parties and feasts—everything!

This isn't a new idea. God called his people Israel to remember him and show the world what he was like through the everyday stuff, the big and the small. The special feasts, which were extraordinary, were meant to remind them that everyday meals mattered as well. Parties are God's idea. During the Israelites' parties and feasts, they were to remind one another that all of life was to be done as an expression of their love for God. God called them to see their celebrations and feasts as an expression of their worship. He wanted them to use something mundane and everyday—eating—as a reminder that he is to be the center of all the everyday stuff.

God is brilliant, isn't he?

He wants us to see that all of life, every aspect of it, is a good gift from him. He wants our hearts to cry out, "God is so good!" in the middle of everyday life. He wants us to eat, play, create, work, celebrate, rest, and relate to one another for his glory. God always intended that every part of life be a participation in his activity in the world and a celebration of his goodness to us all. So he told Israel to do all the stuff of life—working, resting, eating, and celebrating—in remembrance of him.

I love this about God!

I grew up believing that after I died, I would go to heaven, which would be like an eternal church service. As a teenager, I wasn't too excited about that. All I could imagine was a bunch of us in white gowns floating on clouds that felt like hard wooden pews. We would forever listen to long sermons and sing songs from red hymnals. Later in life, as I read the Bible, I found out that this is not an accurate picture of our future with Jesus. The Scriptures tell of a day when we will dwell on a new earth and enjoy a sin-free existence, living life fully and abundantly with God in our midst. We will eat, play, create, work, celebrate, and rest in perfect harmony with God and one another. It will all be good and it will all be worship!

Imagine if the church was like this now.

God's Calling to Israel

That was clearly God's desire for Israel. While the whips of Egypt were still fresh in their memories, God reminded his people that he had delivered them from slavery and would be in their midst continually. He commanded them to eat a meal (the Passover) to regularly remind them of how he had rescued them. But he didn't end there. He also commanded them to throw several other kinds of parties that would tell the stories of his love and provision for them. In fact, God not only commanded Israel to party in his name, he also required that the people give a significant portion of their money to make sure the celebration was done well.

Can you imagine churches today taking offerings so they would be known as the people who threw the best parties?

God wanted the nations to know what he was like by looking at Israel's celebrations and feasts. He wanted the other nations to want to belong to Israel because the best of life is lived in God's care and under his leadership. He wanted Israel to be a people who pointed forward to a new world, where life would be lived perfectly together. They were to be a foretaste of the future reality so that all nations would want to join them in it one day.

God didn't want just Israel as his people in the new world.

He wanted all peoples, every tribe and tongue, all the creative expressions of every culture, together worshiping him through every aspect of life.

It didn't happen.

The people of Israel failed. They didn't make God the center of the party.

Their parties and festivals became empty rituals—passionless religious events. God wanted them to love him and others through the everyday stuff. However, they let the everyday stuff of life become mundane. Sure, many of them continued to observe the feasts, but their hearts were not in it. At one point, God told them that he hated their parties and feasts because their hearts were not directed toward him.

Can you imagine how sad a day that must have been? The invitations have been sent. The decorations are hung. The food is prepared. The guests arrive. Then God arrives; after all, the party is for him. But imagine that he tells you he hates the party. He hates it because you have forgotten to celebrate him. He hates it because every aspect of your celebration tells a lie about what he is like. The party doesn't demonstrate his character and desires. And it clearly doesn't show how much he loves people. It is a Godless, loveless party. And he hates it!

That's what God did to Israel. They forgot about him, not just at their feasts and festivals, but in the stuff of everyday life as well. Their celebrations and life together became merely empty rituals. They did not love God and they did not love the people he sent them to bless.

God doesn't just want us to feast or celebrate as his people. He wants us to remember him, keeping him central to the party by showing kindness, love, and mercy to all those who lack a reason to celebrate. We are to be the "good-news people" to the world, who show the good news in our lives and invite others to receive it into theirs. The celebration is to be for God. The party is to be about God. After all, it is meant to tell the world what he is like.

The Israelites forgot who they were and why they had been called to be God's people. Their feasts became empty, heartless, ritualistic events. They were partying without the life of the party, celebrating without a reason to celebrate. That led to self-absorbed consumption and heartless activities without love.

The same can happen to us if we forget to keep God central. Church becomes an empty, heartless religious event.

Jesus Redeems the Party

So Jesus came as God in the flesh to show us the heart of God for people. Before Jesus did any formal ministry, he spent thirty years of his life doing normal, mundane, unremarkable stuff. He lived a regular life for the glory of God. He ate, played, learned, celebrated, worked with his hands, and rested just like the rest of humanity. Think about this! God moved into the neighborhood, and nobody but a few shepherds took notice. And they did so only because a bunch of angels showed up while they were watching their sheep and told them to go see Jesus.

Jesus lived a normal, quiet life for thirty years in an unknown town. He was so normal that when he began his public ministry, the people from his hometown couldn't believe it. "Isn't this Jesus of Nazareth?" they asked. "Isn't he the carpenter's son who lived among us, doing normal stuff like the rest of us?" (see Matt. 13:53–58). The difference is that Jesus did everything for his heavenly Father's glory. He lived all of his life as an expression of his love for God the Father. Jesus did what Israel didn't do. He did what we don't do. He set apart every aspect of life as holy unto God.

That is what the word *holy* means—"set apart."

God first sets people apart for himself. He makes people

holy. It is his job, not ours. We can't make ourselves holy; only God can do it. He did it with Israel. God set Israel apart as his people and made them holy. However, they failed to set apart life unto God. They became a holy people living unholy lives.

Jesus was set apart for God in the world, and everything he did was to glorify God. He was holy, and every aspect of his life was holy, because he did it unto God. When he ate, he blessed God for good provision. When he worked, he knew he was doing it unto God and showing off the creativity of our Creator. He submitted to authority humbly and gladly as an act of submission to God, who ordains rulers in every place. He served, shared with, and loved others because he knew God is a serving God who gives good gifts and is love himself. Jesus lived every part of his life in submission to God. Every action was an act of love to God and others, and every one of his thoughts was directed by God. Jesus lived a fully God-dependent life. Holy Jesus lived a holy life wholly unto God.

Finally, after thirty years of quiet, submissive, humble worship, Jesus began to publicly proclaim the good news of God's kingdom—that there was a new order to things, and he was going to bring all of life under God's authority. He wanted a holy people who would live all of life wholly unto God. God was making a way for all of life to be restored to the way he always intended it to be. Everything could be made good and all of life could be worship. Life could be as it was always meant to be!

But Jesus didn't just proclaim the good news. He lived a good-news life, showing what God's rule and reign looks like when God breaks into the normal stuff of everyday life.

So Jesus went to a party.

It was a wedding feast in Cana. They had been celebrating and partying for days, so the wine ran out. How embarrassing this was for the bride and groom, as well as their families!

So Jesus's mother came to him for help. Jesus then ordered the servants to fill six jars used for ceremonial cleansing with 120 gallons of water. He then turned the water into wine—and Jesus's wine was better than every drop they had consumed earlier. Jesus entered into the events of everyday life. Then he took the ceremonial stuff of religion, changed it, and made the party better.

This is what Jesus does. Jesus makes life better. Jesus brings the better wine. He takes empty religion and ritual, and brings it to life for everyday people. He takes what many deem holy (like the water in the ceremonial cleansing jars) and brings it to the party. He breaks down the barrier between what people might call sacred and secular. Jesus makes all things sacred—including wine at a party.

Don't miss this.

Jesus is giving us a picture of what God is like. Jesus is the Word of God made flesh to bring the life of God into our wine-less (worshipless) party. The holy Word became human flesh. The holy God became holy man. The holy shows up in the mundane when the mundane is set apart for God's work in the world. God became flesh and dwelt among us. Water became wine and satisfied the thirsty at the party.

Jesus did this so that we also could do this.

He came to rescue a people back to God so all of life would be seen as sacred; all of life would be set apart unto God; and everyday stuff would be seen as worship—even a poker party.

A New View of Church

The idea of everyday stuff done for God's purposes in the world had gotten Greg's attention.

"Brett told me you guys are starting a church," he said. "But you don't seem like church people. You're hosting a poker party!"

I thought about what Greg had said while I stared down at my hand, trying to keep my poker face on. Greg had grown up in the church, but he had vowed never to go near one again. All he saw when he looked at the church was an empty, lifeless, loveless institution with structures and events. He rejected the church because he hadn't experienced the love of Christ there.

For Greg, church seemed disconnected from everyday life. He observed people *doing* church, not Jesus *living life* through his church. In his mind, church had become merely a religious event.

Greg and Mary were also struggling in their marriage without much relational connection to others for help. On top of that, Greg was personally struggling with a lack of purpose in life. At that moment, they felt hopeless and helpless.

Brett had been sharing with him our vision of church as the people of Jesus living intentionally together on mission in the everyday stuff of life. Brett had been inviting Greg to come to our dinners and parties for a while, but Greg had continued to refuse. He held onto his belief that the church was not something he could be a part of. But Brett was changing, and Greg could no longer ignore this. The two of them had grown up together as friends, but something was different. Brett was different. Could there be something to this church that Brett was talking about?

So Greg came to the party.

"Many people have the wrong view of church," I said to Greg. "They see the church only as a building or an event they go to on Sunday. Others see the church as the leaders or pastors who put together programs for its members. That's why, when people say, 'I like or don't like such and such church,' they are actually referring to the way the leaders or pastors lead, teach, or organize the people. They don't usually mean they like or don't like the people."

This wasn't the first time I had explained what the church is. Several times over the previous six months, I had pulled out a napkin at a coffee shop or restaurant, drawn a picture of a church building, and described how most people have this wrong view of church in their minds.

"Some think it's a building you go to," I would say as I drew a picture of a building. "Others think it's the programs and events that happen there [here I would draw circles inside the building, representing activities], while others think it's mainly the leaders who run those events [at this point, I would add some stick figures inside the building]. They think the job of those leaders is to get people to invite their friends to the building [here I would draw stick figures and arrows pointing toward the building]. They also encourage people to give their time [I would draw a clock], their money [a dollar sign], and their skills and gifts [a gift-wrapped present] to support what happens primarily in the building."

Next, I would draw arrows going out of the building. "Though we might gather together in a building," I would say, "the church of Jesus is the *people of God saved through the person and work of Jesus Christ for his purposes in the world.* God's intent was never to have us define church merely as an event on Sunday. We don't *go* to church. We *are* the church sent out into the world." Then I would draw stick figures, a clock, a dollar sign, and a present beside the arrows coming out of the building.

Then I would say: "Jesus wants us to live all of life fully for his glory in the world—every part and every person. Jesus didn't live, serve, suffer, and die so we could just attend a Christian event. He lived and died so we could become his people who are sent into every part of the world on his behalf. He wants all people everywhere to see and know about him, and he wants everyone to know that everything is to be done for his glory. We now see our time, our money, and our unique abilities as means to serve both the people who are the church and those in our cities who don't know the great news of God's love for them in Jesus Christ. All of life counts and everyone matters.

"You have a teaching gift? You may use that to teach people who gather as the church weekly. However, what if you also used that ability to serve in the public schools as a teacher? Maybe you're a gifted administrator. Think about how many places in our city need strong administration! Or maybe you're great at building businesses. What if we started businesses that existed to bring good to people and cities as a way of show-ing what God is like and that he really cares about commerce as well?"

I would continue to demonstrate how every person and every gift could be used to show others what our God is like in the world. I would also describe how the majority of our time and resources should not be poured only into our gatherings of Christians. We are blessed to be a blessing to our world with all God has given us. He wants to pour us out as an act of his love to the world.

People have a hard time seeing the church this way, because they see life in terms of the sacred and the secular; they think of things as Christian or non-Christian. They believe some things or events are good and godly, and others are not. They de-fine *things* or *events* as Christian or secular—such as Christian music or secular music, Christian fellowship or secular parties. They see a church gathering on Sunday as sacred or Christian, but not the rest of life. That's why they dress differently, talk differently, and often act altogether differently at "church" on Sunday than they do during the rest of the week. And those who are not yet a part of the church or have left it want nothing to do with it because it doesn't seem to have anything to do with the rest of life.

However, the Scriptures don't define church or Christians this way. Neither do they define life this way. It's not activities and events that are primarily Christian. It's people. Activities and events, by themselves, are not sacred, but people are.

As we saw earlier, the word *holy* in the Bible means to be set apart for God's purposes in the world. God's desire was never to have a people who are separated from the world, creating some kind of Christian cul-de-sac. He wants every part of life to reflect his greatness. He wants his people doing all of life for his glory everywhere, so that the world becomes surrounded by the life of God that is in the world through his people.

What makes an event or activity sacred is not calling it "Christian" or inviting only Christians to it. Something is holy unto God when God's set-apart people do what they do for his glory: eating, drinking, playing, celebrating, working, resting, creating—you name it, God wants us to do all that we do for his glory (1 Cor. 10:31). For example, there is no such thing as truly "Christian" music. Music isn't Christian, people are. However, when Christians, who are set apart for God's work in the world, make music for God's glory, it is sacred.

Jesus at the Center

Over the poker table, I continued to share a vision for church that was very different from what Greg had heard before.

"The role of Jesus's church—his set-apart people—is to increasingly bring all of life under his leadership so that he is the center of everything," I said. "We are Jesus's people (the church), who go to work with him and for him. We are Jesus's people, who eat with him and for him. And we are Jesus's people, who can party and should party with Jesus and for Jesus. He wants to fill the city of Tacoma with his presence through his people in everything and in every place. He is here with us right now because he loves to be present among his people at the party. We are Jesus's church living for his purposes right now."

I went on to describe how, as Jesus's church in Tacoma, we planned to lead people to Jesus and then train them in how to live all of life for him. Right there in the middle of the game, we all started to dream about what a church that embraced all of life lived for Jesus's fame might look like. For instance, we started to dream out loud about how business could be done for the good of our city and the fame of Jesus. "What if we ran businesses that served our city and made a lot of money to serve those in need at the same time? We could show our city that our God is generous and compassionate." We brainstormed for a while on that theme and many others.

I think I was beaten pretty badly at poker that night, because I got so caught up in the vision of normal people like Greg, Brett, and others being the church in the everyday stuff of life. As I reflect on that time, I am amazed at the creativity and passion released in these men as they dreamed about their role in seeing all of life done with Jesus and for Jesus in our city.

That same creativity is in you and your friends as well. If you have God's Spirit, you have the One who created the universe in you. Have you ever taken time to dream about what God might want to do in and through you where you live and work?

We did.

Our core group started seeing everyday life as the place where God wants to work through his church. We threw parties, ate together, and joined in with the activities of our city. We taught Christians to see themselves as the church in our city, instead of seeing church as only an event they attend on Sunday. They learned how to see all of life as sacred and every action as part of God's missionary work in the world. They began to see that he was in them, working through them in the normal stuff of life. They began to go to work as people on Jesus's mission, hung out at the park on mission, and celebrated in homes, pubs, and coffee shops together on mission. We served neighbors, schools, and various social-service organizations. We cleaned city parks and walked the city streets while praying. We ate together often and celebrated God's grace in our lives.

In all of this, we sought to experience and show what God is like in the everyday stuff of life. As a result, more people were drawn to Jesus and his community, and more people engaged in everyday life for God's glory.

I have found that one of the main reasons many people do

not get involved with the work of God in this world is because they don't believe God wants to or can use them. They don't know that Jesus prefers normal, weak, and broken people.

Like my dad, many wrongly believe that God's work is mainly done in a church building by a few paid professionals, and that the members of the church are primarily needed to volunteer to run the programs and provide the financial support. Normal stuff doesn't count, because God doesn't work in the normal stuff, they believe. They can't imagine themselves on his mission in the world, because they have wrongly believed God's mission isn't in the world. Church seems so disconnected from the rest of their lives. Clearly, God can't use them, and therefore he must not want them.

But this is simply not true. God loves to use normal people in the everyday stuff of life. He wants everyone involved in all of life.

All In

That night over a game of cards, Greg's heart was captured by the thought of being called to Jesus in all of life. He could actually see how following Jesus would change how he lived his life. Jesus was pursuing Greg at the party. He wanted to work in and through Greg to bring change to our city. Greg began to believe there was a place for him in this. Jesus wanted his life, his skills, his passions, and his daily activities. Greg didn't need to become a pastor, teach Sunday school, go to Bible school, or run a church program to be a significant part of Jesus's work in the world. Greg needed to come to Jesus, place his faith in what Jesus had done for him, and surrender his life to Jesus. Then Jesus would work through Greg wherever he went, to show the world what Jesus is like and tell them who he is and what he had done in Greg's life.

"I'm all in!" Greg said, as the poker chips tumbled forward into the center of the table.

Something had happened in Greg and Mary that night around poker, feasting, drinking, and talking together. On the way home, they said to each other, "We've got to be with those people again!" They could see God wanted them. Jesus was building his church, and it was looking different than they expected. Maybe there was a place in it for them as well.

There's a place for you too. Jesus wants to work in and through your life, all of your life, including the everyday stuff.

God brought Greg and Mary back to himself through Jesus working through his body, the church, at a party. He also brought healing and health to their marriage, and eventually God called Greg to take leadership of an organization called Network Ministries—a transitional ministry that helps move homeless families into homes where they are trained for life. Greg and Mary came to Jesus through the normal stuff of life, and now they train others how to live all of life submitted to Jesus.

As we struggled to find a name for this people—the church Jesus was building us to be in Tacoma—we finally landed on Soma, a Greek word that means "body." In Ephesians 1:23, the apostle Paul calls the church Jesus's body (his *sōma*), through which he fills all in all. Paul's vision, given to him by the Holy Spirit, was of the church being the body of Christ, through which Jesus fills every place with his presence through his people.

All God's people, everywhere, filling everyday life with his presence.

This is the vision that captured our hearts as well. We are Soma—Jesus's body, through which he intends to fill every place with his presence so that every person might have a daily encounter with him in every way. Jesus saturation—Jesus filling every place with his presence through normal, everyday people in the everyday stuff of life. This has always been God's vision for his people.

Please consider joining us and many others around the world as God fills every place in every way with his presence.

But make sure you start with Jesus.

We can't do this without him.

Part 2

Jesus

3

Jesus Is Better

The day had started off well. It was a dry, warm morning in the Northwest, and I was up early to play a round of golf with some friends. I had my morning coffee in hand and was enjoying the sound of birds in the background, while in the foreground I could hear the collision of club meeting ball. It was pretty quiet on the fairway, peaceful and serene.

But the scene was very different in my heart.

Ryan, Todd, Ray, and I had begun golfing together fairly regularly. When people asked if I was a golfer, I always responded, "No, but I golf." Ray and I were basically on par in our abilities, while Todd and Ryan tended to outplay us.

This particular day, Ryan was going on and on about our need to better care for the children who were part of Soma. We were a couple of years into our journey as a church, and it seemed more children were being born all the time. As many children were part of our church as adults. It was clear that some changes had to be made in how we led our children and families.

Now, I don't know if Ryan was bringing up these concerns because they really were on his mind or if he was just scheming to take me out of my game. If it was the latter, it worked. I started slicing my drives and duffing my fairway shots. I usually was great on the green, but even my putting was falling apart. All I could think about was everything that was wrong with our church. Ryan didn't know it, but there were a dozen other problems on my mind as well. His concerns served to top off the barrel of my heart, and it started to overflow with anxious thoughts. It wasn't quiet inside me. I wasn't at rest.

We were all running as hard and fast as we could on mission: hosting cookouts with neighbors, serving our schools, feeding the homeless, partnering with the arts community, starting small businesses, meeting with politicians, fixing homes, and caring for families whose spouses had been called to war. It seemed we were doing something every night, and the pace was wearing us down. We wanted to see our whole city saturated with the good news of Jesus, but making it happen was turning out to be much more overwhelming than we had expected!

On top of that, we had walked through some terribly heart-breaking situations.

Shortly after we welcomed our second child, Caleb, into the world, Jayne's dad passed away from cancer. It was September 12, 2004, the same night we commissioned our first four missional communities (officially the launch of Soma). We had trained smaller groups of people to live as the church on Jesus's mission in the everyday stuff of life, and now they were ready to begin doing it on their own. What should have been a hopeful, expectant, vision-casting night was overshadowed by the deep pain of our grief. I was praying over four groups of leaders while Jayne was at her dad's bedside, saying goodbye.

I loved Bob! I couldn't believe he was not going to get to see the work come to fruition. And Caleb would never get to know Bob. He would have loved Grandpa Bob!

On top of that, a student from Willow Creek who was like a little sister to me had committed suicide. I was devastated. Then, a month or so later, a young couple we had helped get off the streets, and who were beginning to consider Jesus and his claims, gave birth to a stillborn baby. I will always remember holding this lifeless baby in my arms as I prayed with this couple. A few days later, I found myself officiating the funeral and overseeing the burial.

"This isn't going the way I had planned! Is something wrong?" I remember thinking.

Next, we watched a couple's marriage disintegrate right in front of us. They were part of our core! We found ourselves spending night after night with people desperately in need of counseling.

We were engaged in very real spiritual warfare. At times, it was against our daughter; at other times, the core members were under attack.

I was so tired and frustrated. I was feeling very discouraged and weighed down with all the pressure and demands of broken people.

And I wasn't the only one who was tired and overwhelmed. It turned out that many others who had joined us on the mission were feeling the same.

So there I was on the twelfth hole, setting up for what is normally an easy shot for me, a hundred-yard iron shot to the green—and I completely duffed it!

"That's it. I'm done! I can't take this anymore!" I said as I threw my club. It must have gone at least twenty yards farther than the ball I had just hit.

The guys had never seen me react like this, so they were

stunned. Sure, I was competitive, but I didn't throw clubs! I was a mess; I couldn't hide it any longer.

"What's going on?" they asked.

Trying to Be Jesus

At this point, any attempt to cover up would have been futile, so I began to describe everything I was going through. I went on and on about all that was broken with Soma—and with me. We had been driving hard toward mission with a broken-down car, and now the engine was overheating, the gauges were going crazy, and the wheels were coming off.

Ryan, Todd, and Ray stopped golfing and created space for me to be heard—and for me to hear. Mission will squeeze you and the junk will come out. When this happens, you need others to walk you to Jesus. That's what my golfing friends did for me that day.

Todd reminded me that this mission was not my work: "It's not your church, Jeff. It's Jesus's. The weight doesn't have to be on your shoulders. Jesus said *he* would build *his* church."

I think Ray made some joke to try to get me to laugh: "Don't worry, at least Soma's not as bad as your golf game!"

"You're not helping, Ray," I replied, half crying and half laughing.

In that moment and in the following weeks, the Holy Spirit showed me that I had been trying to carry the weight of Jesus's mission on my shoulders, and, in turn, I had been putting it on everyone else's shoulders. I was asking them to be and do something they couldn't be or do.

I was trying to *be Jesus* and I was asking them to *be Jesus*. But we can't be Jesus. Only Jesus can be Jesus.

Our job is not to *be Jesus*. Our job is to believe Jesus, depend on Jesus, and submit to Jesus working in and through us to accomplish his work. We are not meant to carry the weight of the world or the mission of Jesus on our shoulders. Jesus came to seek and save. He doesn't expect us to become the saviors.

Have you ever done this? Have you ever tried to be a savior, to save someone? Are you carrying a heavy burden that only Jesus is meant to carry?

As you consider *being the church* on mission where Jesus has you, as you think through how to bring the gospel in word and deed to the everyday stuff of life, please know that you cannot do this alone. Yes, you need to do it with a community. But above all else, you need Jesus. All of us do.

Jesus is better than any strategy. He is more faithful than your promises. He is more able to bring real, lasting, heart-level change. He is the greatest missionary ever.

Jesus is better. He's better than you. He's better than your small group. He's better than your pastor. He's better than anyone or anything else.

I had forgotten this.

Letting God Be God

In Romans 1, Paul describes how we all exchange the truth of God for a lie and exchange worship of the Creator for worship of his creation. As a result, our minds become foolish and our hearts become dark. God turns us over to our worship of false gods, but they don't give us what we really want and need. So we lust for more. We want them to do what they can't really do for us, so we demand more from them. This lust is at the heart of all addiction. It's at the heart of all of our brokenness. We've all done it and we still do it.

In other words, we take a good thing and demand that it be a "god thing" for us. We do this with sex, friendships, food, alcohol, work, and even our children and spouses. Then, when God gives us over to our passions, we pervert or try to control our "god," twisting it, distorting it, and ultimately destroying what it was meant to be for us. God lets our sin and idolatry have its final way with us, so that our minds become twisted and we think, believe, and do all kinds of destructive things—tearing ourselves and others down (Rom. 1:18–31).

God lets us have life with the god we think will save us or save others, and it always fails. He wants us to know that no other person or thing can be God for us as he can and no other person or thing can save as he does.

That's what God did with me. He let me try being god for a while. He also let me put the weight of being god on our church. Both failed.

I needed to be reminded of who the true God was for our church, for our city, and for my family. We all needed a true and better Savior than me.

It's interesting: I came to Tacoma to bring a message of the good news that Jesus saves, but I believed and lived out a message that Jeff saves. That wasn't good news at all.

I desperately needed Jesus. Our church needed Jesus. After all, Jesus said, "Apart from me you can do nothing" (John 15:5). Sometimes you have to fall apart to figure this out.

Over the years, I watched many others try to do the work of Jesus without looking to Jesus to do the work. I also watched people look to a pastor or leader to be Jesus for them. Some looked to a particular methodology. None of that works.

Whenever people tell me they're going to move to Tacoma to join what we're doing here, I tell them: "This is a lot like Oz. You think you're going to follow the yellow brick road, singing and dancing along the way, and trusting that at the end you will find your answer or solution. However, you are going to find that we are no different from you. We are just like the wizard behind the curtain. We are just as needy as you are. Soma isn't what you're looking for. Missional communities are not the new Savior. What you need, what you're looking for, is Jesus.

And if you don't already know him, believe him, and have his Spirit in you, then our job will be to lead you away from us or a program to him. If you do know him, then we will simply call you to trust and obey him, because you already have everything you need. Jesus is not just in Tacoma. He is in you!"

Past, Present, and Future Salvation

When we started, we were not as certain about this as we are now. Sure, we proclaimed the message of the gospel for salvation, but we didn't believe that we, ourselves, still needed it. "The gospel is for those who don't yet know and believe in Jesus," we thought. The gospel, we believed, is primarily good news for your afterlife, not your present life.

At this point, I was providentially introduced to Tim Keller's teaching on the gospel, and how the person and work of Jesus is sufficient not only for the beginning of my Christian life, but also for the middle and the end.

Paul reminded the church in Rome of the confidence we can have in Jesus and his work. In Romans 1:16–17, he writes: "For I am not ashamed of the gospel, for it is the power of God for salvation to everyone who believes, to the Jew first and also to the Greek. For in it the righteousness of God is revealed from faith for faith, as it is written, 'The righteous shall live by faith.'"

The gospel is the power of God for salvation. Salvation from what? What do we need to be saved from?

God wants to save us from the *penalty* of sin—salvation from what we've done; the *power* of sin—salvation for what we're called to do today; and the *presence* of sin—salvation for our future.

It is a past, present, and future salvation. And it's all available to us by faith. We come to experience the effects of God's salvation by believing the gospel.

Paul says that in the gospel, "the righteousness of God is revealed from faith for faith, as it is written, 'The righteous shall live by faith'" (Rom. 1:17). Paul is saying, in essence, that the good news is that God has power to save everyone who walks by faith, believing God can save him or her. The good news is that God saves us as we trust in him and not in ourselves. And the means by which God does this—the righteousness that is revealed—is the life, death, and resurrection of Jesus applied to our lives by God's Spirit.

God is ready to rescue you. He has the power to do it. And he is calling you to come to him for what you most desperately need right now. You need Jesus—for what you've done, for what you're doing, and for what you will do.

Thank you, Jesus, for bringing me to the end of myself on that golf course. I believe it! You're right. I need to believe the gospel of Jesus Christ now for every aspect of my life!

If we're going to be effective in seeing people and places saturated with the good news of Jesus, we first have to know and believe the gospel. We need to be saturated with the truths of the gospel before Jesus saturation can happen through us.

Do you know the good news of Jesus?

Do you believe it?

Do you live as if you believe it?

We all need the better Savior. Jesus is that Savior, for he *did* better than us, he *does* better than us, and he *will make everything* better than we ever could.

The next three chapters are all about the good news of Jesus for you. Let's get saturated with Jesus so Jesus can saturate the places where we live through us!

4

Jesus *Did* It Better:
We *Have Been* Saved

"Explain how this injury occurred."

I stared at the report in front of me as I sat in the waiting room at the urgent-care clinic. I was in severe pain, and my hand looked like a small boxing glove covered with skin. "So, what should I put on this report?" I asked myself. "How about, 'I smashed my hand in a door'?"

It was partially true. It was a door, and I had smashed my hand into it. Actually, I had punched it. Same thing, right?

I was having a rough season, walking through the sinful behavior of one of our leaders and the fallout it had created in our church. On top of that, my schedule had been getting way too hectic. Then Jayne and I got into a fight. It seemed like every button that she knew how to push got pushed. I was angry.

I couldn't help thinking, "It's Easter week; everything should be going better than this." As soon as she left the house, I punched the door.

There's a reason our hundred-year-old home still has its original doors. They are strong, so strong that they don't budge when you punch them.

However, my hand budged. I heard the cracking sound, immediately followed by swelling.

So there I was in urgent care, trying to determine how I should report this injury.

Sin Leads to Brokenness

In Romans 3:23, Paul tells us, "For all have sinned and fall short of the glory of God." To sin is to think, believe, or act in any way that is not like God or in submission to what God commands. We all have fallen short; every one of us has sinned. And "the wages of sin is death" (Rom. 6:23a). The result of our sin is damage to ourselves, brokenness in our relationships, destruction to the world around us, death to our physical bodies, and, ultimately, an eternal spiritual death, separation forever from a relationship with God, the giver and sustainer of life.

Our rebellion, our sin, leads to brokenness—and sometimes to a broken hand.

"But the free gift of God is eternal life in Christ Jesus our Lord" (Rom. 6:23b). God has made a way to give us something different from what we deserve.

Since no natural human being ever has lived or ever will live a life perfectly glorifying to God, Jesus came and took on flesh as the God-man. Jesus became for humanity the true and better human, the true Son of Man and Son of God. He submitted himself perfectly to God the Father. He obeyed him in everything, doing only what God the Father told him to do. This perfect obedience—this perfect life—has been given to us. Jesus is the gift of God to humanity (John 3:16). This is good news!

By faith in Jesus, you and I are saved from the need to live a perfect life to gain God's approval. Paul says that our lives are now hidden with Christ in God (Col. 3:3). That means that if, by faith, you have trusted Jesus as the One who perfectly obeyed God on your behalf, God sees Jesus's performance as yours. He accepts you because of Jesus.

I really needed that good news on the golf course that day with Ryan, Todd, and Ray. Not only did I need Jesus's better behavior exchanged for my outburst of anger, but I also needed to be reminded that the Father did not accept me or love me any less or any more based upon how well I performed on mission. He already loved me perfectly and fully in Jesus, his Son.

Staring at the injury report, I needed the good news again. I needed to know that I could be honest about my brokenness. I didn't need to cover up or lie to make myself look better. "For all have sinned." This includes me. There was no need to perform any longer.

Where are you tempted to hide or cover up? Do you still believe you have to perform well for God in order to receive his loving acceptance? Do you believe God loves you more when you obey and less when you disobey?

You don't need to look elsewhere. God the Father, the Creator of the universe, receives and accepts you in Christ Jesus. If you believe this, you can rest. You are loved. You are accepted. You are already significant!

Hear this also: we need more than Jesus's perfect life of obedience. We also need his death on the cross.

Jesus didn't just live a perfect life for us. He also died in our place. Paul tells the church in Corinth, "For our sake he made [Jesus] to be sin who knew no sin, so that in him we might become the righteousness of God" (2 Cor. 5:21). Jesus took all of our sinful rebellion on himself at the cross so that we would no longer be defined by our sin, but by his righteousness.

By faith in the death of Christ on the cross, all of your sin is paid for and all of your guilt is removed. Jesus died in your place to declare you forgiven and no longer guilty. This was not just for the sins you have committed, but for every sin you will ever commit. Jesus died one time for all—for all who put their faith in him, and for all our sin.

Confessing Our Brokenness

I once met with a young man who was struggling with looking at pornography. Not only was he ashamed about his sin, but he seemed to be controlled by his guilt. These feelings led to an ongoing cycle of hiding, followed by secrecy, followed by more porn watching, and so on.

I asked him, "Do you believe Jesus died on the cross to forgive you of this sin and remove the guilt from you?" He said he was struggling to believe. So I reminded him of the truth of the gospel, that Jesus's sacrifice on the cross sufficiently paid for his sin and removed his guilt: "Every sin you have ever committed or will ever commit was placed on Jesus in that moment. He died for your sin, and that act was sufficient to forgive you and completely remove all your guilt. When Jesus said from the cross, 'Father forgive them, for they know not what they do,' that also was applied to you." We prayed that God's Spirit would help him to believe this, and gradually he did.

Then I asked him how long it generally took for him to go from the act of looking at porn to satisfy himself to returning to the foot of the cross to receive grace from God and be reminded that he was already forgiven and accepted. He said it sometimes took days. I asked him whom he was putting his confidence in—whom he was worshiping—during those days in between. He said, "Well, I guess me."

"That's right," I said. "I want to encourage you to try something. Next time you look at porn, immediately get on your knees and thank Jesus for dying for what you just did. Thank him for his grace and forgiveness."

"I can't do that!" he replied.

"Well, what gives Jesus more glory in your life? You trying to pay for your own sin through your loathing and self-hatred for several days, showing you don't believe that what Jesus did on the cross was sufficient to deal with your sin? Or being so convinced of the sufficiency of Jesus's death that you can go straight to the cross in that moment as a reminder that Jesus's death was enough—that Jesus really is that incredible and his grace really is that amazing?"

He said, "Clearly Jesus is more glorified in the latter." Then he went on to say, "If I did that, I don't think I'd want to continue looking at porn, because I would be so overcome by his grace instead!"

"That's exactly right," I said. "It is his grace that teaches us to say no to sin."

While staring at the injury report, I needed that same counsel. My first thought was to cover up. I was feeling self-hatred and shame. But God's Spirit would not let me go into hiding. He reminded me again that Jesus had died for this outburst of anger. He had already forgiven me at the cross. There was no more guilt, no more shame, and no more need to hide or cover up.

"I punched a door," I wrote on the report.

I continued to fill out the report until I got to this question: "Who is your employer?"

"Really?" I thought. "Are you kidding me? I don't want to give our church a bad name. I could just put 'Soma.' It would be honest and no one would know it was a church."

Then the Spirit reminded me again of Jesus. That's his job,

by the way—to keep directing us to Jesus. Jesus is not ashamed to call me a brother, nor is he ashamed to associate with a church full of broken people. If our church were to gain a reputation of being full of people who need Jesus's grace, well, that would be great!

If we don't believe we need the gospel, we will not believe the gospel. If we don't believe the gospel, we won't proclaim it either.

So I wrote down "Soma Church."

Phew! That was over. I turned the report in. "Now," I thought, "let's get those X-rays."

Later, when I saw a doctor, he asked, "So, how did you do this to your hand?"

"Really? You can't read?" I thought. "You've got the charts. I already wrote down how I did this!"

To keep calm, I rehearsed the all-important truths in my mind: "Believe the gospel. I am forgiven. I can boast about my need for a Savior. I don't have to lie, hide, cover up, or be ashamed. I am not ashamed of the gospel—the same gospel that affirms that I was a sinner who needed Jesus to die for me."

So I said, "I punched a door." It actually came out of my mouth.

Next, it was on to the X-ray technician. And she asked, "So, how did you do this to your hand?"

"Again?"

Finally, the doctor who wrapped my hand in a cast asked, "How did this happen?"

"This is not going to end!" I thought.

I found out later that they all likely knew what I had done since this particular injury is called a "boxer's fracture." They'd seen plenty of them, and a medical professional only needs to look at it to know what happened. I guess they just wanted to see if I'd confess it out loud.

God Uses Weak Things

Something happens when you confess your brokenness out loud. In order to confess it, you have to believe it first: "I am broken." Then you have to humble yourself to say it.

Sometimes I think we believe we have to have it all together to be effective on mission. Actually, the Scriptures tell us the opposite. First Peter 5:5–6 tells us: "'God opposes the proud but gives grace to the humble.' Humble yourselves, therefore, under the mighty hand of God so that at the proper time he may exalt you." God loves to use the weak things of the world to show his greatness (1 Cor. 1:27; 2 Cor. 4:7; 12:9–10).

The confession continued. Everywhere I went, people asked about the cast: "How'd you do that?" It actually became quite hilarious how often I had to humble myself and tell the truth. The Spirit of God was sinking the beautiful truths of the gospel deeper and deeper into my being every time.

Jesus saturation was happening to me.

Remember, this was Easter week. I still had to get up on Friday and speak at Soma's Good Friday service. The irony: in order to get up and preach the gospel, I had to believe it for myself.

Thankfully, it was dark at the Good Friday service because the lights were down. Even so, I don't know if I've ever been more mindful of my need for the cross of Jesus on a Good Friday. I needed grace. I needed a Savior.

Finally, Easter came. There was no darkness, no hiding my cast. It was bright, and everyone could see the cast as I stood up to proclaim that Jesus is risen from the dead.

So I told the story and confessed my need for Jesus's forgiveness. I boasted in my need and his sacrifice for me. I preached with authority because I knew personally that the gospel works. It really is the power of God for salvation.

Jesus died—I am forgiven.

Jesus rose again and lives in me—the broken me.

I didn't need to hide. I raised my cast up high and told everyone: "I need a Savior. I need Jesus. And I am not ashamed of the gospel, because it is the power of God to save someone like me!"

Just as I need a Savior, you do as well. Today. Right now.

Have you trusted in Jesus's life and death yourself? Are you still trusting in it? Do you believe that what he did was sufficient for you? Do you believe Jesus perfectly lived in your place, and that he humbly and sufficiently died in your place?

Disciples of Jesus do believe this. We have to. We can't live the life he calls us to apart from it.

Are you striving to gain approval or acceptance? Rest in Jesus's perfect work on your behalf.

Are you living with regret or self-hatred for what you've done in the past? Accept Jesus's payment for sin.

Are you striving to do enough good now to remove the guilt of the bad you've done in the past? You don't have to. In fact, you can't do enough. Instead, believe that Jesus has fully removed all the guilt from your life.

We have all sinned, but Jesus did better for us. Because of him, we are forgiven and cleansed. We are loved and accepted by God.

We all talk about what we love most and what we believe has affected us most. So if you love and believe in Jesus, raise your broken hand high and boast in Jesus. You must believe it if you're going to tell others about it.

He *did* it better than you!

He also *does* it better than you.

5

Jesus *Does* It Better:
We *Are Being* Saved

"I know it's wrong. I just can't stop," she said.

"You can't or you won't?" Jayne asked her.

We were meeting with a woman who had recently come to faith in Jesus, but who had continued to engage in behavior that was marked by sinful unbelief. She knew what was right, but she would not do it.

"I can't. I just can't go there. Can we stop talking about it?"

Jesus didn't come and die just to forgive us of our sins, leaving us helpless and powerless to live a new life. He rose again and is alive to enable us by his Spirit to live a whole new life.

This woman believed she was forgiven of her sins, but she was still trusting in her own ability and power to live her life.

I had been doing the same thing leading up to that day when I threw my golf club.

Go back with me to the church in Corinth. These believers had begun to question whether there was a bodily resurrection from the dead—whether people will be given new bodies to live in in a new world one day. This was huge! If people are not raised from the dead and given new bodies, then what happened with Jesus? Paul tells them our entire faith is futile if there is no resurrection (1 Cor. 15:12–19).

Paul confronted their wrong thinking by reminding them of the gospel: "Now I would remind you, brothers, of the gospel I preached to you, which you received, in which you stand, and by which *you are being saved*, if you hold fast to the word I preached to you—unless you believed in vain. For I delivered to you as of first importance what I also received: that Christ died for our sins in accordance with the Scriptures, that he was buried, *that he was raised on the third day* in accordance with the Scriptures, and that he appeared to Cephas, then to the twelve" (1 Cor. 15:1–5).

If we have faith in Jesus to save us, we have been saved and we *are being saved*.

Paul uses the language of *being saved* in describing what the gospel is still doing. Yes, the gospel is good news about a past event—Jesus lived and died in a definite time in history to forgive us of our sins. Yet the gospel is also good news about what God continues to do in us and through us.

Jesus was raised from the dead on the third day. He is alive! He lives for us and, by his Spirit, he lives in us and works through us.

This truth is absolutely key to Jesus saturation happening through us!

His resurrection showed that he had put death to death. He overcame sin for us, raising us from spiritual death to spiritual life, and he disarmed the spiritual rulers and authorities that held us captive, making us slaves to sin (Col. 2:15). The same power that raised Jesus from the dead is now in us who believe. Therefore, we can live new lives of love and obedience, free to submit to God in everything, just as Jesus Christ did (Rom. 8:1–11). We can live the life God created us to live in the first place.

Jesus is the firstfruits of a new creation. Just as Adam and Eve were given a world over which to exercise authority and to fill with humans who would take care of it, Jesus is the new Adam and his bride is his church—all of us who have come to him in faith. Jesus and his church will one day live forever together on a new earth that is perfect and without sin, brokenness, or death. At this point in time, however, Jesus is the only One who has the new body for the new earth. And he is dwelling in his people by his Spirit. That means the perfect future can break into our present brokenness. The life and power of Jesus to live a new life is available now.

The Future in the Present

Did you ever see the movie *Back to the Future*? At the end, the eccentric inventor Doc Brown comes back from the future to warn Marty McFly. The Delorean time machine comes flying out of the sky and lands in front of Marty's home. Doc gets out and begins urging Marty to come with him back to the future: "It's your kids, Marty. Something's got to be done about your kids!" In the movie's sequel, Doc takes Marty into the future to see what is going to happen so he can return to the present and raise his children differently. He goes to the future so that he can live in the present in a whole new way.

Jesus is doing a similar thing for us, except that the future world we are headed toward is better, not worse. Jesus is the future reality for all of us who have entrusted our lives to him. One day, we will be like him (1 John 3:2) and will live in a perfect world with him. In the present, he comes into our lives by his Spirit to give us a glimpse, a foretaste, of the future so that we will live differently today. As we trust and depend on him to work in us, he enables us to live the new and better life now.

Let's go back to the day when I threw my golf club in an outburst of anger. At that time in my life, I was living as if it was all up to me. I believed I was saved. However, I was living as though I had to be the savior of our church, of our neighbors, and of our city. I was not believing that God was still in the act of saving us through Jesus, who is alive in us right now. I was not believing the gospel. I was depending upon *my* strength, *my* skills, and *my* ability to inspire, persuade, influence, and lead. Because of that, I was living the old life and not experiencing the new life Jesus can make possible in me.

Unfortunately, I was calling our church to try to live a new life without Jesus's life as well. I called them to go and "be Jesus" to the people in our city without depending on the power and presence of Jesus. How crazy! Trying to be Jesus without Jesus working though us is not the life he rescued us to live. It's not a life of faith. It's a life that will crush you under its weight of impossibility.

Remember, Paul said, "The righteous shall live by faith" (Rom. 1:17). Faith in what? Faith in the Son of God who is alive in us.

Listen to Paul's words in Galatians 2:20: "I have been crucified with Christ. It is no longer I who live, but Christ who lives in me. And the life I now live in the flesh I live by faith in the Son of God, who loved me and gave himself for me."

What did I need to do on that golf course? I needed to believe the gospel for my present, not just for my past or future. I needed to believe that Jesus is alive and living in me today, able to do all the work he wants to do in and through me, and able to do the work he wants to do through our church family as well. He wasn't asking us to try to be like him without his power and presence. He was asking us to let him work in and through us.

This is how Jesus saturation works—Jesus in you and working through you.

The woman with whom Jayne and I were meeting needed to believe the gospel as well. She needed to believe that Jesus didn't just die for her sins, but also that he rose again and was present and able to empower her to live a new life by his Spirit.

We shared Philippians 2:12–13 with her: "Work out your own salvation with fear and trembling, for it is God who works in you, both to *will* and to *work* for his good pleasure." Then I said: "I know you believe you can't do this. You're right. Jesus said that apart from him we can do nothing (John 15:5). You can't do it. But he can. Jesus is more than able to work in you to change your desires and your ability to do what he wants. Do you believe that?"

"Well, I think so, but I don't want to go there," she responded.

"So, you don't even have the desire at this point to do this? Then, how about we start here? Jesus is able to work in you to *will*—that means he can give you the *want to*, the desire. Are you open to starting there—asking God to change your desire?"

"Yes, I think so," she responded.

So we stopped and prayed. She asked Jesus to change her desires through his Spirit.

I have to let you know that this woman struggled in this area until she recently passed away. She had a hard time believing that God was powerful enough to save her from this brokenness. She continued to try to do it on her own, in her own strength. She now knows how powerful God is and how present and real Jesus is. I would bet that if she could, she would tell all of us to stop living as if we were still slaves to sin. There's freedom and power in Christ to live a new life. Live it today!

Cease Striving and Let Jesus Work

Maybe you're like she was. Are you stuck in a pattern of sin? Do you believe you can't live a new life? Are you struggling to believe that God can save you from the power of sin now? That he has the power to enable you to have new desires and new behaviors?

"I've tried. Really, I have," you might say.

Stop trying on your own. Cease striving and acknowledge that he is God and you are not. Don't try to change your desires or your behaviors without him. That is the work that only God can do in you. Invite him—Jesus, the living Savior of the world—to come and do his work in you and through you. Salvation is about him working in us both to give us his desires *and* his abilities—his passions and his power.

Simply say: "Here's my life, Jesus. Do your work in my life. Do your work through my life."

I still forget this. I find myself slipping back into "Jeff Mode," looking to myself to change me and to change others.

Even as I have been writing this chapter, the Spirit has been showing me how hard I've been striving with all of my own energies. I've been thinking: "I want to write well. I want this book to change people's lives. I don't want to fail at this. It's too important!" The Spirit keeps telling me: "Don't do this without me. I'm better at this than you are. Let me lead you. I will give you the words. Trust me. I want to change people's lives and I want to do it through your life. But it's got to be us, Jeff. Not just you. You can't do it without me."

We have not just *been* saved. We are *being* saved by Jesus today—he is alive and he is at work in us right now.

Jesus *does* it better than you. And he wants you to do it with him, with his power and his presence.

Stop and invite him to actively save you today in the areas of your life where you are still trying to do it on your own. He is faithful and he is powerful.

Invite Jesus to be your present salvation now.

And know that he also *will make* it better than you can.

6

Jesus *Will Make* It Better: We *Will Be* Saved

Before I resigned from my position at Willow Creek Community Church, I was nearly paralyzed by fear. I experienced many sleepless nights filled with anxious thoughts. I found myself praying during the commute to my office just so I could face the day and lead our team. I had to fight my way through the day. Then I prayed all the way home so I would have something, anything, to give to Jayne and our newborn child.

Fear is an interesting thing. It's not about what is happening. It's about what we believe will happen. It's connected to what we believe about the future.

Have you ever been so afraid of the future that you were paralyzed in the present? That's where I was.

I was struggling to lead our team because I had lost their

trust over a key decision I had made. During this time, a leader of the church told me that if I didn't perform well at Willow Creek, I might never get a job in ministry again. He told me that churches were looking to us, and if they saw me fail, they likely wouldn't hire me. I think this leader thought this conversation would motivate me.

Fear *does* motivate. It just doesn't always have the desired result. In my case, fear didn't push me forward with unbridled resolve. It bound me in shackles.

Seeking help, I was meeting with a counselor at this time. He asked me, "What are you afraid of?" I remember telling him I was afraid of never being able to work in the church again. He asked me, "Who do you believe has the power to bring that about?" I gave him the name of this leader, since he was such a powerful man in my mind.

My counselor then helped me to see that this man was just that—a man. I had allowed a man to become a god to me. I believed he held my future instead of God. I feared losing my job, and this leader had the power, in my mind, to ensure I'd never get a job in the church again. So his approval became everything to me. And my fear of losing his approval had a controlling power over my heart.

I don't blame this leader for inducing fear in me. I couldn't see it clearly at that moment, but I was responsible for my fear. I had put my trust for the future in the wrong savior. I believed that this leader was holding my future. I had an unbelieving heart. I needed to believe the gospel again. Once I saw my unbelief and was set free of it, I was able to die to self and to the approval of man. It was in dying to unbelief that I truly found freedom to live.

We won't see Jesus saturation happen through us if we are captured by fear. I'm convinced from my experience that people will not step out on mission if they don't have confidence about the future. Their fears control them.

A Secure Future

What you love most, you also fear losing the most. And whatever threatens what you love most controls you.

Parents love their children. I certainly love mine very much. However, if I love them more than God and his mission, I will build my entire life around them, and then I will be controlled by a fear of anything that could threaten them. I have watched many parents walk away from obeying God for fear of what it will do to their children. They refuse to engage in mission with those who don't know and believe in Jesus because they have more confidence in people's ability to influence their children than the gospel of Jesus Christ and his Spirit.

I once spoke with a couple who had many children whom they home-schooled. They told me they had become convicted that they had made their children the center of their world. The reason they home-schooled, they confessed, was because they were afraid of the world. They also had refused to allow their children to have any contact with the neighboring families because of their fear. As a result, they had disobeyed Jesus's command to make disciples of all peoples. They confessed this to me. They wanted to change and submit to Jesus, and to submit their children to him as well.

I reminded them that Jesus cared about their children more than they did. God was a better parent than they were. He loved them and was watching over them. I assured them that if they wanted to obey Jesus together as a family, he could be trusted with their future. They agreed, so they repented of their idolatry of their children and surrendered them back to God. They also told me that they believed they needed to ask their neighbors to forgive them for isolating themselves from them. When we met again later, they informed me that they had hosted a party for all their neighbors, during which they told them they were sorry for living in isolation. God opened many doors for the gospel as they stepped out in faith in the One who holds their future.

This doesn't just happen with our children. It happens with our jobs, our dating relationships, our marriages, our finances, and our retirement plans. What we love most has controlling power over us.

I loved the approval of man and feared losing that approval. I also believed it was all up to me.

That is why the writer of Proverbs says, "The fear of the LORD is the beginning of wisdom" (Prov. 9:10), and why Jesus tells us that loving the Lord our God with all of our being orders everything else rightly (Matt. 22:34–40). We love God because he first loved us. He loved us by sending the Son to satisfy his just wrath against us for our sin. So we have no need to fear judgment coming against us for our sin. Perfect love casts out fear (1 John 4:7–21).

First Peter 1:3–5 tells us that God "has caused us to be born again to a living hope through the resurrection of Jesus Christ from the dead, to an inheritance that is imperishable, undefiled, and unfading, kept in heaven for you, who by God's power are being guarded through faith for a salvation ready to be revealed in the last time." Not only do we have no need to be afraid of future judgment if our faith is in Jesus, but we also have no need to fear loss. Our salvation is kept in heaven *for us*. Also, Jesus is presently at the right hand of God the Father, representing all those who have faith in him. He is securing *us* until the end. And he has all authority in heaven and on earth (Matt. 28:18). The thing that matters most cannot be taken away from us, and nothing can happen to us to prevent us from inheriting it.

Our relationship with God, our future salvation, and our hope to live eternally with Jesus on a new earth are already secured.

If our faith is in Jesus to save us, we have been saved, we are being saved, and we *will be saved*.

Jim Elliot was a missionary who was speared to death in 1956 while trying to evangelize the Huaorani people of Ecuador. One of his most well-known quotes is this: "He is no fool who gives what he cannot keep to gain that which he cannot lose."[1] He had been set free from the fear of losing his life, because he knew the One who had secured his eternal life.

A New Future

Scripture also tells us that in the future, God will make all things new. All sin will be eradicated. All that is broken will be restored. Every person who belongs to Jesus will be healed. All relationships will be reconciled. We will enjoy a perfect world with Jesus at the center forever. It will be stunningly amazing!

Jesus doesn't just hold and secure our future. He gives us a perfectly new one as well.

One of the most important things my father-in-law, Bob, said to Jayne while he was dying of cancer was this: "Jayne, this world has nothing to offer you. Don't run after the things of this world—you run after Jesus!" This dying man had an understanding of what really matters. He knew that anything done apart from Jesus is futile and temporary. He died with his eyes fixed on Jesus, the author and perfecter of his faith (Heb. 12:2).

He lived like it, too. I watched Bob step out to share the love of Jesus with his actions and his words to many people. Bob began his new life of faith with his eyes fixed on Jesus, and he ended with those same fixated eyes. At his funeral, I met people from all backgrounds and faiths. Not all of them shared Bob's

---

[1] *The Journals of Jim Elliot*, ed. Elisabeth Elliot (Old Tappan, NJ: Fleming H. Revell, 1978), 174. Entry from October 28, 1949.

love for Jesus, but every one of them spoke of a courageous man of love who did not hold back in fear but gave his whole heart to everyone he met. I loved this man! And what I loved most about him was his love for Jesus! He truly knew who held his future, and he believed it would be better than anything we've experienced here.

I'm writing this while on an airplane. I'm crying in front of everyone as I think about Bob's love for Jesus, but I don't care what people around me are thinking, because this kind of love for Jesus is so compelling.

That is what the apostle Paul says in his second letter to the Corinthian church, after describing his confidence in God's ability to secure his future. Some were questioning Paul's authority and calling, but he was not afraid of them. He says:

> Therefore, *knowing the fear of the Lord*, we persuade others. But what we are is known to God, and I hope it is known also to your conscience. We are not commending ourselves to you again but giving you cause to boast about us, so that you may be able to answer those who boast about outward appearance and not about what is in the heart. For if we are beside ourselves, it is for God; if we are in our right mind, it is for you. For the *love of Christ controls us*, because we have concluded this: that one has died for all, therefore all have died; and he died for all, that those who live might no longer live for themselves but for him who for their sake died and was raised. (2 Cor. 5:11–15)

Paul knew that in the end, God will have the final word. Therefore, he feared the Lord above men, and the love of Christ controlled him more than anyone or anything.

If we believe that Jesus is the Savior of our future—that he is the one who holds us in his hand, and that he will keep us until that day and will only make it better—we can rest secure in him even in the middle of this broken world where we live.

The Better Savior

Do you believe God holds your future? Do you believe he is better than anyone or anything else at securing your tomorrow?

I want to encourage you to place your trust in Jesus as the One who can secure your future. Let him have your greatest affections and your most confident hope. He is the only One who can secure our future salvation. No one is greater than him. No one can take away what he holds. You are safe in his hands and have no need to fear. If you believe this, you can join with Paul and say, "For me to live is Christ, and to die is gain" (Phil. 1:21).

In order to step out into God's mission to see Jesus saturation happen, you have to believe this. Fear of any other paralyzes you. But the fear of the Lord and the love of the Lord set you free to live a wildly courageous life of radical love for others.

You need to believe the gospel in order to step out and obey Jesus.

You need to believe he *has* saved you. You are forgiven and loved; there is no record of wrongs against you.

You need to believe he *is* saving you. You can do all things through Christ who gives you strength.

You need to believe he *will* save you. You have nothing to fear because your future is in his hands.

Jesus really is the better Savior!

He *did* it better.

He *does* it better.

He *will make* it better.

Part 3

Discipleship

7

All-of-Life Discipleship

"So how can we be sure we're not joining some crazy cult?" Ray asked Jayne and me, while our firstborn, Haylee, who was at the crawling stage, busily harassed Ray and Diane's dog. Ray and Diane had invited us over to hear more about the church we were starting.

Ray reminds me of Popeye.

He had been in the Navy, and was short but strong, a little rough on the edges but soft on the inside. Ray is a jokester and a straight shooter. For that reason, I'm sure his question was partly about having some fun with a young church planter who desperately wanted a few older people to join a small, inexperienced core group. However, the question also revealed how far removed he (like many others in the church at large) had become from a biblical understanding of what it means to be Jesus's disciples.

I had recently spoken at Ray and Diane's church, and they had joined several others after the service to hear me present our vision for being the church in Tacoma. During that time, I shared the vision of seeing every part of Tacoma filled with the presence of Jesus working through everyday people in everyday life. "Jesus didn't come to earth, take on human flesh, live among people as the Servant of all, suffer, and die so that we could just 'go to church' for a couple of hours a week," I shared. "No, he wants it all. He wants all of our lives all of the time. He wants to fill every place with his presence through his people. He wants *every* person in *every* place doing *everything* to glorify God. Just as when Jesus called his first disciples to follow him, when he calls people to be his disciples today, he intends it to be an all-of-life kind of thing that affects everything."

This sounded like a cult to Ray. "All of life!" he thought. "Everything? Really? Is this guy serious?"

However, when you consider Jesus's life and ministry, this vision isn't surprising. When he called the first of his disciples, he said, "Follow me, and I will make you fishers of men" (Matt. 4:19). They had been fishermen, but Jesus was calling them to fish for people. They responded by leaving everything—their families, their careers, their futures—to follow Jesus. It started in a boat and went out to the world. Those first disciples radically recentered everything in their lives around Jesus, his teaching, and his mission. Their lives became all about Jesus! He was that important to them.

Then, after he had trained them for more than three years, suffered and died for their sins, and risen from the grave, Jesus told them to meet him on a mountain before he ascended to heaven. On that mountain, he was going to give his final commission to them to make disciples of all people groups. Just as Jesus had called them to follow him, be changed by him, and obey him, he planned to send them out to call others to follow him as well. He was going to send them to the ends of the earth so that Jesus saturation might happen.

So they met Jesus on the mountain and worshiped him there, but some still doubted (Matt. 28:16–17). They were in, but not all in.

Slow down and don't miss this.

Jesus's disciples had seen everything they needed to see. Jesus had taught them all he needed to teach them. And they had experienced all they needed to experience with Jesus! And yet, some were still doubting.

This is good news for me! Though I've walked with Jesus for more than twenty-four years, I still struggle with doubts. Maybe you do as well.

We're not alone! The disciples were still in process—a process that would last their lifetimes. And the same is true of us.

That is what discipleship is all about. It is the ongoing process of submitting all of life to Jesus, and seeing him saturate your entire life and world with his presence and power. It's a process of daily growing in your awareness of your need for him in the everyday stuff of life. It is walking with Jesus, being filled with Jesus, and being led by Jesus in every place and in every way.

A New Perspective

Part of the reason Ray asked if we were a cult was that no one had ever walked him through what all-of-life discipleship looks like. He had never been commissioned to go beyond the Sunday service and join Jesus in filling every place and activity with his presence. This sounded far more intrusive and expansive than what he'd ever heard Christians called to do.

Maybe it's new to you as well.

Maybe, like many, you have believed that being a disciple of Jesus is primarily a one-time decision you make at some point in your life. Maybe you went forward at a church gathering and joined some others in praying a prayer as someone guided you. Or perhaps you raised a hand to signify you wanted to trust in and follow Jesus.

If so, you might be thinking right now, "So, I am a disciple, right?"

Well, yes. But discipleship doesn't end there. Now that you've come to Jesus, you must continue to walk with him (Col. 2:6–7), become acquainted with his ways, and grow up to become more and more like him in everything (Eph. 4:11–16).

Jesus didn't call us to merely make a decision for him. He doesn't need our vote of approval. He doesn't want deciders. He wants disciples—people who are devoted to becoming more and more like him in everything, everyday.

Or maybe you thought being a disciple of Jesus is primarily about what happens after you die. You want to be with him forever alongside many others who love and worship him. So you put your trust in him for your afterlife.

Good. But that's not all there is. Jesus doesn't just want your afterlife. He wants your present life. He wants to live in and through you, changing you day by day. He came to give you abundant life now, and that life is found in him (John 10:10).

But here's the kicker: you have to shift from the passive idea that it is someone else's responsibility to grow you up to be more like Jesus. You need to take your own discipleship seriously. If you love Jesus, trust Jesus, and have Jesus's Spirit, you can start to grow up in following him and becoming more like him yourself.

Feeding Oneself

In one of our conversations, Ray tried to remind me of my job as a pastor. He said: "Jeff, your job is to feed me! That's what a pastor is supposed to do." I remember thinking in that moment: "Really? You want me to feed you like a mother feeds her infant?"

Ray didn't make up this idea. I'm sure he was taught it in church gatherings and possibly even read about Jesus instructing Peter to do this. After he rose from the dead, Jesus told Peter, "Feed my sheep" (John 21:17). Jesus was referring to the lost sheep of Israel, who needed to be fed, like infants, the pure milk of the gospel message of God's pursuit and rescue of his people through Jesus. Peter had been with Jesus. He had been trained to digest Jesus's teaching and give it out again in the form of easy-to-digest "milk" to those who were going to become newborns in the faith. Peter no longer needed someone to feed him milk. He could feed others. Eventually, those he fed would grow up and become able to feed others as well. This is what disciples of Jesus do—they make disciples who can make disciples.

The early church experienced struggles in this area. People weren't growing up. Hebrews 5:12–14 says: "For though by this time you ought to be teachers, you need someone to teach you again the basic principles of the oracles of God. You need milk, not solid food, for everyone who lives on milk is unskilled in the word of righteousness, since he is a child. But solid food is for the mature, for those who have their powers of discernment trained by constant practice to distinguish good from evil."

This conversation with Ray sparked a memory of traveling with Jayne from Seattle to Chicago on a train. At one point, a boy who looked to be about six years old walked up to his mother and said, "I'm hungry, Mom!" I expected her to pull out a bag of snacks or a piece of fruit and give it to him. What we saw next shocked us. The mother lifted up her shirt and the boy began to drink his mother's milk right there in the middle of the aisle! That six-year-old boy was being breast-fed.

Is this what Ray was asking me to do in a spiritual sense?

Those who don't yet believe the gospel of Jesus *and* those who are new believers in Jesus certainly need someone to feed them. They are spiritually unborn or newborn. Those who are at this stage still need someone to digest the Word of God and give it back to them in an easy-to-digest form. This is spiritual milk.

Maybe this is you. That's OK. Seek out mature disciples of Jesus to bring the basic truths about Jesus to bear on your heart and life. You need milk, and God wants to feed your soul with the truthful words about his Son, Jesus, found in the Bible.

On the other hand, those who are maturing in the faith are increasingly able to digest the Bible's teaching themselves. They have come to know, embrace, and love Jesus and all he has done for them. They know how to read the Bible and discover the good news of Jesus found throughout it. They can eat solid spiritual food.

Feeding Others

But it doesn't end with eating. As Christians mature, they come to see it's no longer just about them. They are able to digest the Bible themselves and give it out in the very simple form of milk to those who are still children in the faith. They act much like a mother who eats solid food and gives it to her baby in liquid form.

"Are you still a baby?" I jokingly responded to Ray. Since he was a straight shooter, I could be pretty direct with him as well. "How long have you been a Christian, Ray?"

He responded, "Around forty years."

"So, after forty years, do you still think you need someone to feed you? Don't you think you should be able to feed others by now?"

The truth is that no one had ever trained Ray to make disciples using the Word of God. I'm sure he had read the Bible. But there is a big difference between just reading it and obeying it. Another key difference is being able to teach others to read it and obey it as well.

After years and years of faithful service to the church, Ray did not know how to feed others. He was not a rebellious church member. He gave, attended, heard great preaching week in and week out, and served as an usher. Yet Ray didn't think he could feed himself and others the Word of God. The idea of being the church sent into the everyday stuff of life to make disciples was not only new to him, it was a bit intimidating.

This is one of the reasons we Americans are not making as big of an impact in our country as we could. Most American Christians still believe they have to bring their friends to hear their pastor teach the Bible and proclaim the gospel. But a large percentage of people in our country will never go to a gathering on Sunday to hear someone preach. If we are going to fill every place with the gospel in word and deed, we need to take seriously our own discipleship and ability to study, know, and teach God's Word.

I encouraged Ray to start with a very basic practice. I suggested that he read his Bible every day, asking God's Spirit to guide him into the meaning of what he read and inviting the Spirit to lead him in what he should do. I instructed Ray to write down what he learned as he read the Bible and what God's Spirit told him to do in response. I reminded him that the same Spirit who inspired the writing of God's Word was also with him to enable him to understand it and apply it. "Listen to God's Spirit through God's Word," I told him. I wanted him to obey the Spirit and then teach someone else what he learned.

Read, listen, and obey—then pass it on.

To help him grasp what I was suggesting, I took Ray to the account of Jesus with the woman at the well in John 4. I showed him that Jesus, responding to his disciples' concern that he hadn't eaten anything, told them: "I have food to eat that you do not know about. . . . My food is to do the will of him who sent me" (vv. 32, 34). Then I promised him that if he would listen and obey what the Spirit led him to do, he would be better fed than through any sermon he had ever heard.

I'll never forget his response: "Well, I don't know if I agree with you, but I will try it for a week. If it doesn't work, remember, it's your job to feed me."

When Ray came back to me in a week, he was amazed. He told me he'd never had a better week. He had learned, he had listened to the Spirit, and he had done what the Spirit had told him to do. As a result, he had discovered that partnership with Jesus in everyday life is extremely fulfilling. He was eating a full-course meal served up by God's Spirit.

Over the next year, we helped Ray join Jesus on his mission to our city in the everyday stuff of life, and eventually Ray went from being a Sunday server and observer to a discipler of men coming out of homelessness and addiction. He also started pouring his life into young men who lacked fathers to show them what God the Father is like. He learned to feed himself, and then began to feed others.

It's never too late. We watched Ray and Diane grow to minister to others in their own unique ways. Young or old, God wants you to be a part of his work of making disciples.

Three Key Environments

God is alive. He is present by his Spirit. He has given us his Word so that we might know all we need to know in order to love, trust, and obey Jesus. He has given us his Spirit so that we can be guided into the truths we need to know and be given direction and power to do what he wants. He will lead you if you will submit to him. He will guide you if you will listen to him. And he will feed your soul deeply if you will heed his Word and obey what he leads you to do (John 14–16).

Over the course of several years, as we've grown in following Jesus daily and helped people like Ray increasingly submit to Jesus in everything, we've discovered that this kind of discipleship cannot happen simply by attending church gatherings or going to classes. Certainly these can supplement people's discipleship process, but alone they are insufficient. All-of-life discipleship—learning to follow, trust, and obey Jesus in the everyday stuff of life—requires submitting to and obeying God's Word in three key environments: *life on life*, where our lives are visible and accessible to one another; *life in community*, where more than one person is developing another; and *life on mission*, where we experience making disciples and, while doing so, come to realize how much we need God's power.

The next three chapters will help you understand why these environments are so important and how you might engage in a more wholistic approach to discipleship.

8

Life on Life

"I'm so mad right now!" Randy exclaimed as he perched high on a ladder, filling holes on the south side of our house with putty. Randy was a former Army Ranger platoon leader who had seen three tours of duty. He had recently become a part of our community on mission.

A few months earlier, I had noticed that our house was ready for a new coat of paint. One day, while I was examining the siding, I noticed a loose piece and gently pulled it away from the house. The gap revealed another layer of siding hiding beneath the present facade. The previous owners had covered up all of the original beauty and craftsmanship of our home, built in 1911, with a plain, flat facade. I never would have noticed this had I not gotten close enough to peel back the outer layer.

Sometimes the stuff that's underneath the outer facade of our lives never gets revealed. It's there, all right, but it's hidden underneath the layers of performance and platitudes that we've learned to fasten over our real selves. Someone needs to get close enough to see that there's something underneath and then to peel back the facade—gently, of course, with loving grace.

I decided that we should tear off the new facade of our house to repair and restore the original. But Jayne warned me that this would be much more work than I could ever imagine. I'm a visionary, which means I am often a little too optimistic and less realistic. However, I don't mind asking for help, so I told her, "That's OK, we can ask our missional community to help."

She said: "They aren't going to want to help us. That's too much to ask." Jayne felt it would be self-serving for us to ask for help with home repairs. She was struggling with the idea that humility is expressed only in serving others, not in letting others serve you.

Some of her facade needed to be peeled back as well.

"They can always say no," I said. "Let's at least ask." So I presented it to them. They were a little overwhelmed by the size of the project, but eventually they all agreed.

So there we were, three months into it. Jayne had been right! This was much more work than I could ever have imagined. But it was also good for us. The work on the house became a metaphor for what all of us were going through personally. Every piece we removed revealed more brokenness and wear. "There was a good reason the previous owners covered this all up!" I started saying over and over again. "It's a lot easier to cover up brokenness than to restore it."

But what is broken is still broken even after it is covered up.

Covering up our brokenness, hiding our need for restoration, is much easier than the actual restoration. Or so it seems. The problem is that we're still broken. Covering up doesn't change the problem. It just masks it so that not everyone can see it.

However, God sees. He knows. And he is not satisfied with the cover-up. He wants to restore you to his original design. That is what discipleship is about—making you truly human, just as Jesus is the perfectly complete human.

His means of restoration is others in your life who are committed to bringing your brokenness out into the open and bringing the gospel of Jesus to bear on it. The layers with which we've covered ourselves have to be pulled back, and we can't do that kind of work alone. We have to get close. We have to be seen and known.

This is what we call life-on-life discipleship—life that is lived up close so that we are visible and accessible to one another, so that others can gently peel back the layers and join us in our restoration.

Exposure Leads to Restoration

Jesus spent more than three years with his small band of disciples, eating, working, celebrating, and serving. They were up close and personal with him. They watched him in every possible situation. They saw what it looked like to submit to God in everything because they saw Jesus do it. He was with them and near them.

He could watch them, as well. He could see the cracks in their facades and pull back the layers. He knew where they struggled to trust God—where life was still all about them and not about submission to God. He often slowed down to draw out their hearts, point out their unbelief, and call them to trust him in every area of their lives.

Jesus lived life with his disciples. He was close enough to really know them. He observed what they believed by watching how they lived. He became closely acquainted with their brokenness so that he could see their wrong thinking, wrong believing, and wrong acting. They were exposed. And as they were exposed, Jesus helped them to be restored.

Randy was being exposed on the side of my house. He was angry. "Why?" I asked.

"No one showed up to help," he replied.

"But why does that make you mad?" I asked. With this question, I started to slowly peel back a layer.

"Because I am all alone!" he exclaimed.

"So why does that bother you so much?" I continued, peeling a little bit more.

"Because they said they would be here and they're not here."

"So, you're angry because they didn't keep their word?" I asked. By asking him to clarify, I was inviting him to join me in peeling back his layers.

"Well, I don't think that's it."

"What is it then?" I wanted us to get to the heart of Randy's anger—the layer below the layer.

"Well, I'm all alone out here."

"I know. Why is that a problem? Why are you angry about doing something alone that you already agreed to do." We were getting there, getting to his heart; the broken part of Randy was about to be exposed so he could be re-formed and restored.

"I guess I'm angry because no one knows. No one is aware. I'm not getting noticed and I'm angry about that."

The facade was removed. Randy's heart had been revealed and his need for Jesus was clear. At last, we could get after the discipleship of Randy's heart, bringing the truths of Jesus to his heart. This was a key discipleship moment.

"Randy," I said, "remember, you are not alone. God is with you, watching you, working with you on the side of the house. And he notices. The good news is that he loves you even if you don't do this. In fact, he loves the guys who didn't show up as well. You don't need to do this work to gain God's love. You already have it because of all that Jesus has accomplished for you. You are loved and accepted in the same way God the Father loves and accepts Jesus. So work for him, knowing that he already accepts and loves you. Don't work to get his love. Work because you already have it."

We continued pressing this truth into Randy's heart right there on the side of the house as he continued to press putty into holes in the siding. At one point, we stopped to pray and ask God's Spirit to enable Randy to really know this truth deeply.

If we are to be disciples of Jesus who are being re-formed and restored to become more like him, we need to have people in our lives, up close and personal. We need people who can see where we do or do not yet believe the truth about Jesus and what he has done for us. Then, when the layers are pulled back, we need people to speak the truth of the gospel to our needs. Sometimes we just need a reminder of what we already know but have forgotten. Sometimes we need a bit of new information about Jesus. And there are times when we need a direct rebuke.

We cannot do this in a classroom. It can't happen in an hour or two a week. We have to get into one another's lives, and it is messy, intrusive, and uncomfortable. At times, it hurts. It's not easy. But if we are devoted to Jesus and leading others to Jesus in all of life, it is worth it—it changes us and others, leading us to become the restored people Jesus wants us to be.

Discipleship Anywhere

Discipleship can happen at any time—while applying putty on the side of a house, cleaning up a yard, hanging out at a party, playing board games (the brokenness is pretty obvious for those of us who struggle with being overly competitive), enjoying a vacation together, watching sporting events, or cooking a meal.

As I was talking through this chapter with Jayne, she recalled an interaction she once had with a young woman who lived with us for a while just after college. Life-on-life discipleship often happens in the midst of relational conflict. Jayne had experienced this, so I asked her if she would write this in her own words:

> We had two small children at home. The single young woman who was living with us at the time was devoted to healthy eating and exercise (my priorities at the time were just trying to get my teeth brushed and a shower by noon). She was a nutrition expert, and often shared what she was learning with me.
>
> For the most part, I welcomed this new information and enjoyed adding to my learning—until, one evening while I was making chicken, I apparently used too much olive oil. She leaned over the stove, glared, and promptly told me that I had way too much olive oil in the pan. I snapped something back at her immediately, but the bulk of my verbal vomit came out later, while we were eating. I really let her have it. I don't remember all I said, but I was mean. I went on a violent discourse, defending my use of olive oil and my deep love and devotion to my family's health and well-being. How dare she accuse me of being a bad mom? We fought as Jeff sat quietly observing, knowing he would *die* if he took a side. She ended up crying and running downstairs to her room. Jeff, our kids, and I were left sitting at the table in a numbing quiet.
>
> "What are you looking at?" I said to Jeff. Then it went to level two of the ugliness. He and I fought as he challenged me to think about what was going on in my heart. I felt miserable inside, and by the end, I knew I needed to talk to her about what had just happened. "Jesus, give me strength!" I prayed. These issues weren't going away, and the worst part was that I knew it wasn't really about the olive oil. It was deeper than that.

So I went down and we talked, cried, and were completely honest about the way we felt about each other. Finally, we were able to hug. While this was happening, I started loving her in a different way. In that moment, God gave me an affection for her, and I realized that I had been afraid of really loving her because I didn't want her to know too much about me. By keeping her at arm's length, looking for a reason to feel justified in my frustration of her infringement on our lives, I somehow felt I was protecting myself from hurt and shame—from really being known.

It's funny, because the things I saw in her that irritated me most were things I didn't like about myself. God was mirroring us to each other. This happens when people get close. Finally, the brokenness inside was coming out. We started to be honest with each other. Both of us had strong personalities and could tend to be harsh. Now we each could see ourselves in the other.

After this event, we were able to extend more grace to each other because we had a common struggle. We were very similar, and it took both of us seeing these weaknesses in each other to force us to address them.

We still know this beautiful young lady and have watched her blossom and grow in grace while still maintaining the strength with which God gifted her. That moment lifted a cloud that had been brewing above us, strengthened our relationship, and made us both more like Jesus.

Most people have been trained to believe that conflict is a bad thing. But we have found that conflict pushes what is already in the heart to the surface. Therefore, it often serves to remove the facade. Living life closely together does this because you can't keep the front up forever. This is what happened with Jayne. Her need for Jesus was revealed. She needed to have more grace for our friend. She needed to be reminded of the grace she had received through Jesus so that she, in turn, might be gracious to our roommate.

The Overflow of the Heart

This kind of stuff also happened with Jesus's disciples. The more he was with them, the more stuff came out. It couldn't be hidden, and Jesus wouldn't allow them to stay the same.

At one point, Jesus said, "It is not what goes into the mouth that defiles a person, but what comes out of the mouth" (Matt. 15:11). He also said, "Out of the abundance of the heart the mouth speaks" (Matt. 12:34). When people live in proximity to one another—when they are around one another consistently— the heart begins to overflow and our internal heart rebellion against God shows up. It's in there, but it's often never seen. This is when the best discipleship begins to take place. This is what Jesus did with his disciples. He didn't just put info in; he drew the heart out. He let the facade fall away so the brokenness could be seen.

In the beginning of my relationship with Randy, he and I met regularly with a few other guys to read the Bible, pray, and learn how to listen to and obey God. Jayne and I also regularly invited Randy and his girlfriend, Lisa, over to eat with us. Eventually, after our other roommate moved out, Lisa moved in to live with our family. We were very involved in their dating relationship, helping them work through their relational brokenness. We also did their pre-engagement and pre-marriage counseling, and I eventually officiated their wedding. Then Randy also moved in, and they spent their first year of marriage living in our home.

When discipling others, it's important to know their story— their background.

As I spent more time with Randy, I came to know his story. He had had an abusive, unfaithful, absent father. As a result, he didn't have a picture of how a disciple of Jesus loves his family well. So part of our discipleship of Randy was letting him watch me as a husband and father. He watched me try to lead family devotions and discussions about Jesus. When you read about discipling your children or sit through a seminar on it, it sounds romantically pleasant—like a Norman Rockwell painting. This has not been my experience. Maybe I'm just lousy at this or my household is a modern version of *The Lord of the Flies*; or maybe discipling children is just messy. Randy had a front-row seat to our mess.

He didn't just see the mess of parenting; he also observed the reality of two broken people trying to be a picture of grace in their marriage. Once, when Jayne and I were having a fight, Randy and Lisa started to get up and excuse themselves. I said: "No! Sit back down! You need to see this. How else are you going to learn how to fight and go to Jesus for help if you don't see it?" So they watched us fight. They heard us raise our voices, watched us cry, and saw grace and forgiveness extended and our relationship restored. They watched us confess our sins, repent, and turn to Jesus many, many times. Over time, they found themselves also able to help us by leading us to Jesus when we were having a hard time going there ourselves.

Randy recalls a time when I was disciplining Caleb, our second child. He remembers Caleb running up the stairs after he had been confronted for doing something wrong. I ran up the stairs after him. Randy told me that when he saw me do that, he thought, "Caleb, you had better run fast because you are going to get hit!" That was all he knew in regard to what a father does when he disciplines his son. He told me later that what happened next forever changed his perspective on being a father.

"Caleb," I said, "you don't have to run away! I love you, son! You don't have to hide. You are safe with me." I pulled him close to me. At first, Caleb was afraid. He knew he had done wrong. In that moment, I reminded him that Jesus had already died for his sin. "Do you believe that, Caleb?" I asked him.

"Yes, Dad," he said.

"If you do, you don't need to hide. You don't need to cover up. You don't need to be afraid. You are forgiven and loved by God the Father! Do you want to talk to God about what just happened between you and me downstairs?"

"Yes" he replied. "God . . ."

"Remember, he's your Father, Caleb. You can call him 'Father' or 'Daddy.'" I regularly tell my children I'm not their real Father, God is. He just brought them into the world through me and placed me over them for a while to direct them to their true Dad.

So Caleb prayed: "Father, I'm sorry for what I just did. I disobeyed my dad. Will you forgive me?"

I told him: "Caleb, you are forgiven because of what Jesus did—he died for your sin. And I forgive you as well. I love you, son. And God your Father loves you very much."

Randy was watching, learning, and being changed. Not only was he being discipled in how to be a father one day, but he was also being fathered in that moment by his true Daddy through me. Jesus was showing him the love of the Father through my relationship with my son.

You can't just teach someone about that. They have to see it and experience it. It requires life-on-life discipleship. You need to be close—visible and accessible.

But discipleship requires more. It also requires a community devoted to one another's discipleship.

$\bigcirc\!\!9$

Life in Community

Randy and I arrived at Seattle-Tacoma International Airport late one evening, coming home from a speaking engagement. A member of our missional community picked us up. Our community had just finished its weekly meal when we arrived. It was my turn to tell my story to the group, and I was excited to share how Jesus had so drastically changed my life. I was hoping that my story not only would encourage our group, but also would lead some in the group to consider trusting Jesus for themselves.

I had just come to the part of my story where Jesus woke me up from my spiritual slumber and rescued me from a life of destruction when Jayne emerged from the kitchen with a plate of food for me. As she set it down in front of me, distracting everyone from what I was saying, she said, "Here you go." I snapped at her: "Can't you see I'm in the middle of something right now? You interrupted me!"

Yes, I did that.

And everyone in the room saw it.

I knew in that moment that I had sinned against God and against my wife. So after the group left, I spoke with Jayne. I confessed my sin of pride. The Spirit helped me to see that in that moment I had believed I was God—that my story, my words would save people. I confessed the sin of pride to God and also asked Jayne to forgive me for how my pride had hurt her.

Our sin does that. Sin is, first of all, rebellion against God. But our sin really hurts people as well.

A few days later, my children and I met Randy and Lisa for breakfast. I could tell they wanted to talk about something. It's often hard for younger disciples to confront older ones in their sin, so I tried to make it a little easier for them.

"Is there something you guys need to talk to me about?" I asked.

"Well, yes—yeah, there is."

"Whatever it is, I want to hear it. I need you guys in my life. And I want you to know you have freedom to speak to me about anything."

They went on to address what I had done at our missional community dinner. I agreed with them. I had sinned. I shared how I had already confessed this to Jayne. Then I asked them to forgive me as well. Next, they asked me to do the same with the whole group the next time we gathered. So at our next gathering, I confessed my sin to the group, and then led them to remember Jesus's sacrifice for our sins through breaking bread and taking his cup together. This led many in our group to confess their sins also. It was a beautiful night of transformation and worship! The community was discipling one another, and each of us was being changed by Jesus.

I need a community. I need to live among people who will

press into me. I still need to be discipled. I'm still in process. Jesus is not finished with me yet, and he has given me a community to participate in making me more like him.

You need it too, you know.

Early in my development as a Christian, I was taught that discipleship happens best through one-on-one meetings. I'm certainly not opposed to one-on-one meetings. However, if you look at the life and ministry of Jesus, and subsequently the ministry of the apostle Paul, you certainly would not come to the conclusion that one-on-one discipleship is best. Jesus discipled his followers while they experienced life together in community. We know they "got it" because the story of how they continued to live tells us they were devoted to one another in the day-to-day stuff of everyday life. Jesus's way of discipleship cannot happen in one-on-one meetings alone.

If I discipled Randy in a one-on-one relationship alone, who would Randy most look like?

Me.

Certainly there are parts of my life that should be emulated. However, it's pretty clear that I have plenty of other areas that are not worthy to be copied. Besides, I'm only one part of the body of Christ.

Who do we want Randy to look like?

Jesus.

Many Parts, One Body

The church is Jesus's body. It has many parts, but it is one body, so it takes many of us committed to Randy's development to help Randy become more like Jesus—*and* to continue to help me become more like Jesus.

We all need many people who love Jesus around us to do this.

The apostle Paul reminds the church at Ephesus that Jesus is the head of his body and we are all parts of his body. Paul describes five different "people gifts" that God gives to the body: apostle (missionary), prophet, evangelist, shepherd, and teacher (Eph. 4:11).[1] Jesus fulfills all five of these roles fully and completely. If we are to grow up into the fullness of our head, Jesus, we need every one of these people gifts providing an example for us, while also encouraging and equipping us.

Apostles/missionaries move outward toward those who don't yet have faith in Jesus, and they encourage others in the body to be outward-moving missionaries as well, both by example and through encouragement and equipping. Prophets have the ability to speak very direct and timely words that encourage or exhort people to remember what God has said and to move forward toward what God wants. Evangelists winsomely draw people toward Jesus and his body, and help others grow in sharing the gospel. Shepherds are particularly designed to ensure people are well cared for and, in turn, care for one another. And teachers have the skill to methodically explain and equip people to know and obey God's Word. When each of these people gifts does what he or she is uniquely designed by God to do, they equip the others to grow up in that ability as well (vv. 12–16).

For example, if one of us is designed by God to be an evangelist, people see his evangelistic activity and fruit, and learn from watching his example as he shares the good news. The training is not just passive, however. The evangelist is also given to the body to proactively train others in evangelism. It is his responsibility to actively help others share the good news of Jesus as well.

Every person in Christ's body is meant to work this way. You are meant to play a part in equipping and encouraging

[1] The Scriptures speak of the original twelve apostles, who were eyewitnesses to Jesus's resurrection, and additional apostles as those the Spirit set apart as "sent ones." I am not implying that present-day apostles/missionaries are the same as the original twelve. Also, there are references in the Bible to God bringing about the writing of Scripture through prophets. I am not implying that present-day prophets are writing or speaking inspired Scripture today.

others. God intends for all of us to actively engage in disciple-making in light of our unique design so that we both do the work and equip others to do it.

Much of this community discipling occurs in our missional communities. It also happens in small groups that meet several times a week for prayer. We call these groups DNA groups because we engage in three activities: *discover*, *nurture*, and *act*.

We spend time reading God's Word, looking to *discover* truths about God's character and activity. We also aim to discover who we were created and called to be, and how that should be worked out through our behavior. We expect to *nurture* one another by asking what's going on in the heart as we discover these truths. We anticipate that God's Spirit will lead us to repentance as we spend time in his Word.

Repentance is turning away from a wrong view or definition of God, or from a person or thing that you have looked to as God, and turning to the true God and the truth about God as revealed in Jesus. Repentance happens when we are ignorant about an aspect of God's character or being, and the Spirit brings illumination to our hearts, leading us to know him in a new way. It also takes place when the Spirit reveals our unbelief about God and leads us to believe a particular truth about God. Lastly, it takes place when the Spirit convicts us that we have willfully rebelled against God, leading us to desire obedience to God in a particular area of our lives.

After we experience repentance, we call one another to faith—to believe the gospel of Jesus. This call to faith in Jesus can come in many forms. In some cases, a person needs to be reminded who God is, as seen through the life and work of Jesus. In other cases, a person may need to have faith in Jesus's power and ability to be and do what she cannot. The person may need to be reminded of Jesus's forgiveness, offered to him through the cross. Or the person may need to be reminded of and encouraged to believe other key aspects of the gospel. In each case, we ask where we need to repent and how the gospel of Jesus is good news for us in this moment. As the Spirit directs us toward Jesus, we encourage one another to believe the good news about which the Spirit reminds us.

Finally, we *act*. Genuine repentance and faith in the gospel of Jesus Christ always lead to changed behavior. So in our DNA groups, we ask: "What action do you believe the Spirit is leading you to take? And who will you tell about what happened in your heart now?"

So we read (*discover*), repent of ignorance, unbelief, or rebellion, and believe the gospel of Jesus Christ (*nurture*). Then we obey and tell someone (*act*).

Changed in Community

Josh came to us full of confidence. He had been trained in evangelism through open-air gospel preaching—the kind where the evangelist stands on a box and, by speaking loudly or with a bullhorn, proclaims the gospel to whoever is passing by. Josh had been trained in a form of street preaching that involved entrapping a person, getting him or her to publicly admit to having sinned, then attempting to lead that person to Jesus.

I won't take time to address the good or bad in this approach. What concerned me most was that Josh didn't know or love his neighbors and had never taken the time to get into people's lives long enough to lead them to Jesus in the everyday stuff. He hadn't been developed well in caring for people (shepherd), engaging in people's lives outside of the church (apostle/ missionary), and taking time to relate the fuller story of God as explained throughout Scripture (teacher). He also needed some strong, direct words spoken into his life (prophet).

Josh joined our missional community. I also invited him to meet with the guys with whom I prayed several times a week, and he was very eager to learn. During our missional community gatherings and our DNA times together, Josh began to realize that he didn't know how to engage in everyday discipleship. Discipleship in community was revealing the areas where Josh needed to be developed and trained.

We had several friends who regularly joined us for our weekly missional community meals. Some of these people did not yet share our faith in Jesus. One evening, Josh and his wife, Dana, participated in a discussion with some of our neighbors who had yet to trust in Jesus. Throughout the night, Josh aggressively argued, counterargued, and cornered one particular couple. The following week, this couple was obviously missing from our weekly meal together. Jayne called them to find out why they hadn't joined us, and they informed her that they no longer wanted to be a part of our weekly meal. When she asked why, they shared that they had been deeply hurt by how Josh had treated them.

At first, Jayne and I wanted to nail Josh. We were angry with him for ruining our mission to our neighbors. Then the Spirit reminded me: "This is the work. You are called to disciple Josh as much as your neighbors."

Being in community together allowed us to see where Josh still needed to be developed. If he had been in only a one-on-one relationship, it is likely he never would have seen the areas where he was still deficient. The community was able to bring a much broader perspective to Josh's life.

The next week, Jayne shared with the group and with Josh about what had happened and why our friends would no longer be with us. She spoke very directly to Josh, and it felt as though God had given her some specific words that Josh needed to hear. It was not easy for Josh. In fact, he was very broken. Josh began to weep. It broke his heart to see that his arrogance and pride had deeply wounded this couple and may have prevented them from coming to know and understand the grace of Jesus.

One of our members described how we might better care for people in the future. Then another led us in prayer for Josh and our neighbors. That moment forever changed all of us. Josh realized that he was more committed to communicating a message about God's love than he was to showing God's love. He also realized that he needed God's love and grace in that moment for his failure. And we had the privilege of leading him to receive it from Jesus.

Eventually, Josh asked our friends to forgive him for how he had treated them. In time, our friends also came to believe and received the grace of Jesus themselves. They saw broken people mess up and receive grace. They didn't just hear a message. They saw people being transformed in community by the gospel worked out in relationships.

This kind of discipleship can't happen in isolation. It also can't happen just by hanging out with Christians.

It requires us to be on mission together.

$$\text{(10)}$$

Life on Mission

Josh and Dana continued to grow in their love for others, both disciples of Jesus and people who had not yet come to faith in Jesus. We watched them begin to reach out to their neighbors and grow in sharing their faith. They were being trained not just in community, but also on the mission of making disciples themselves. The mission revealed their areas of much-needed growth, and while on mission, they practiced what they were learning.

We fulfill the mission of making disciples most effectively when we are on mission in community.

Can you imagine going to a doctor who'd never been through residency training? Suppose you're going in for heart surgery, and just before the anesthesiologist puts you under, the doctor shows up and thanks you for trusting her since this is the first time she's ever done an operation. She assures you she has studied a lot. She was at the top of her class, in fact. She's read every book there is to read on the topic and listened to stories from experts who have been in the field for a long time, but she's never actually done this before. In fact, she's never even been in an operating room before. This is her first time ever. And to top it off, she tells you she's going solo on this first effort. There will be no other doctors in the room!

You pass out. The anesthesiologist doesn't need to do a thing.

Thankfully, this will never happen. A doctor isn't allowed to perform surgery without all the necessary on-the-job training. A full residency is required, in which she begins to apply all of her classroom studies and lab practice under very close supervision. In fact, she observes many surgeries before she is allowed to participate in one. Then, when she does participate, someone guides her and gives constant feedback along the way. During the entire process, she is closely examined and evaluated in order to be properly and completely trained. By the time she enters the operating room to do her first surgery, she has already done many under the close supervision of experts.

Now think about how you've been trained to be a disciple maker. Does the process described above resemble your training? You might say, "Well, with a doctor, we're talking about life and death!" Yes, you're right. And in making disciples, we're talking about life and death as well—eternal life and death. The stakes are high and the consequences are severe! We're talking about people's souls.

We should take the development of disciples—and disciple makers—as seriously as we do preparing doctors for surgery. The residency training we have to offer is the people of God on the mission of Jesus together. To grow toward being a disciple maker in all of life, you need on-the-job training, and that's what life on mission is about.

This is what Jesus did with his disciples. He said, "Follow me, and I will make you fishers of men" (Matt. 4:19). He didn't say, "Show up to class and I will train you." Nor did he say, "Attend synagogue and that will be sufficient." No, he called the disciples to join him on the mission ("Follow me"), and while they were on the mission with him, he trained them to be disciple makers ("I will make you fishers of men").

In other words, Jesus taught them the basics of making disciples while they were on the mission of making disciples.

They could observe everything Jesus said and did. They could see how he rebuked the religious leaders who tried to make it harder for people to come to God. They were able to watch his compassion and care of people being ruined by sin. They couldn't overlook his willingness to heal and help the broken. And the power he exerted over demons was clearly on display. They listened, watched, and learned in the everyday stuff of life. After a while, he invited them to share in some of the work he was doing. Sure, they messed up, a lot, but he was there to help, to correct, to clean up—to train them—while they were on his mission. They were in a disciple-making residency with Jesus.

After the disciples had spent time watching, learning, and practicing under Jesus's watchful eye, he sent them out to begin to practice what he had taught them. He did not send them out alone; they went together. Then they returned and reported to Jesus what they had experienced. All did not go perfectly. So he trained them in the areas of their weaknesses and failures. He did this kind of ongoing training with them for more than three years. As a result, when he finally ascended to heaven, they had been prepared to fulfill the mission.

The best training *for mission* happens while *on mission*.

Formed by the Mission

I used to lead high school students on mission trips. Have you ever been on a short-term mission trip? Do you remember what it was like?

We spent many months getting prepared for one trip to Costa Rica. We learned how to work together. We learned key Spanish phrases ("*Dónde está el baño?*"). We studied the culture and identified appropriate and inappropriate behaviors. We practiced some songs in Spanish and assembled a program using music and mime. We trained the students to share the gospel with others. We also prayed for the work we were going to do. It's fair to say that we *felt* prepared—talked up, prepped up, and prayed up. We believed we were ready to be on mission!

Then we finally arrived at our destination. Spirits were high, but apprehension started to creep in. Anxious stomachs began to rumble. Grumbling, complaining, and second-guessing began.

Later that night, when we all were reunited after visiting our host homes, there was more grumbling: "You should see the place where we're staying! There are bugs everywhere! I'm not sure this food is sanitary. Don't they realize that I have a special diet?" A few days in, some relational conflict arose. People got on one another's nerves, sleep deprivation started to set in, some became fearful, and others grew frustrated: "It's hot. I'm tired. Can I call my parents? This is too much work. I'm sick of so and so."

The facade was being stripped away.

When this kind of thing happened on my very first mission trip, I was caught a little off guard. Back then, I thought the primary mission was the people and place we were going to serve. Through that first trip, I learned that *we* were the ones who were served—God used the mission to change us. That's the beauty of a mission trip. The ones on the mission are often more profoundly impacted than anyone else. The mission happens to them. They go to make disciples, but they are the ones who are changed while on the mission.

The mission itself is God's tool for forming us.

Jesus knew this when he called his disciples to join him on his mission. He knew that the best way to develop his disciples was to send them out on mission. It was while they were on mission together that they realized how little they knew, how little they trusted God, and how selfish and prideful they really were.

While on mission, some of their wrong views of God and his kingdom were revealed. On one occasion, Jesus watched his disciples try to prevent little children from coming to be with him (Matt. 19:13–14). Like many, they thought God was looking for the strong and mighty, the educated and learned, the well-resourced and wealthy. "God needs our help, doesn't he?" they thought. "Why would he want the weak and the simple? They'll just get in the way!" But Jesus peeled back the layers of their hearts to show them what they wrongly believed about God and themselves. He taught them about God's kingdom—how his rule actually works. In the midst of the mission, he taught them that God doesn't need us; rather, we need him. He has all the resources necessary to do his work. Our problem is that we are lacking. We need him and his help. In order to get this—to enter into his kingdom, where we can receive his help and resources—we must become like little children, admitting that we don't have it all together and that we are lacking in resources. The disciples needed to become like little children again. Their mission removed their facade of self-sufficiency.

Mission brings you back to Jesus over and over again because, after all, it is his mission. He will build his church, and therefore his mission is completely dependent on him.

Jesus brings his disciples on a mission that changes them in the process.

That also happened to us on the mission trip to Costa Rica. The outer facade was ripped away and the students' hearts were revealed. My heart was revealed as well. I was shown to be selfish, prideful, and concerned mainly about my agenda. I became tired and easily irritated. My outer facade was torn away, and I was seen for the weak and needy Jeff that I really am apart from Jesus. Our commitments to God were shown to be much more shallow than we had previously realized. Our tendency to trust in ourselves and our preparation instead of God's Spirit could no longer be ignored. It was clear: we were all broken, insufficient, and in great need of help. We needed Jesus! We need help from his Spirit!

And God is present and able. The Spirit of God is our Helper.

Exposed by the Mission

If you are in a small Bible study group, one of the best things you could do is move the study out into the neighborhood. When you read a command in Scripture, ask, "How are we going to obey this command together on mission?" In other words, ask yourselves what this passage says you should do together (life in community) and how you might do it in the middle of a mission field together (life on mission).

Doing this will bring up all sorts of opportunities for discipleship: excuses will be expressed, fears acknowledged, lack of confidence or courage realized, and inadequacies verbalized. Then you'll be getting somewhere in terms of people's discipleship.

In this process, you will discover the truth about everyone's present state. When you actually get out of the comfort of your Christian community and onto the streets of mission (in your neighborhood, at a café, in the park, or at a local high school), you will discover together where everyone still needs to be discipled. The junk will come out, and then you will be able to disciple one another in the everyday stuff of life.

I was surprised by this on my first mission trip, but after a few of them, I knew it was coming. Soon, a part of me began to hate taking mission trips because I knew things would get bad—we would fall apart and we would be seen to be needy.

Yet that was why I continued to lead them. Such brokenness has to happen if real discipleship is going to take place.

Sometimes I wonder if this exposure is why Christians avoid getting on the mission of making disciples together in the stuff of everyday life. We know we will be exposed. We will be seen for the needy, desperate people that we really are. Our junk will come to the surface. Yes, we can hide and pretend to have it all together while sitting in a large gathering on Sunday or while impressing one another with our knowledge of Scripture in a weekly Bible study. But out on mission, the need for grace and power from God will never be more clearly manifested.

That's exactly what we need. We need to see and know our need for Jesus. We need to see and know others' need for Jesus. Then we need to give one another the truths of Jesus to change us, empower us, and allow his Spirit to effectively work through us.

With each subsequent mission trip, I knew that we would come to know and experience God in new, fresh, and powerful ways when it got bad; when we became exhausted and got on one another's nerves; when we just wanted to go home. When it happened, we turned to Jesus together. The students prayed like never before. We remembered the grace we had received through Jesus, and we forgave one another, encouraged one another, and were empowered by the Spirit. As a result, we all grew. We grew in our love for God and one another. Our confidence in God's power and presence increased. We experienced God using weak, tired, and broken people to do amazing work!

This happened in the early church as well. Before Jesus ascended into heaven, he told his disciples to wait for power from God—the Spirit of God was going to come upon them and empower them for the work (Acts 1:8). The disciples were sent out with God's power and presence with and by his Spirit. They faced persecution. Many died for their faith. They lost possessions and family members. Many messed up and grew in the grace of Jesus as a result. And they grew in their love for one another, their devotion to obey God's Word, their prayerful dependence on God, and the powerful proclamation of the gospel. They all grew *while on mission* (Acts 2:42–47).

The mission revealed their need and required God's help!

I'm amazed at how often Christians want to experience the presence and power of God apart from the mission of God. I'm also surprised at how many people believe they can grow people up toward maturity in Christ apart from getting them involved in the mission of making disciples.

This stuff can't happen in a classroom. It does not happen in one-on-one meetings. And it does not happen if we just hang out together as Christians all the time. We have to get out on mission in order to fulfill the mission of being disciples who make disciples.

I used to think we should take people out on mission trips once or twice a year. Now I'm convinced we need to help people see that they are on mission all of the time.

Unfortunately, many disciples of Jesus don't get beyond seeing church as just attending an event on Sunday or Wednesday or doing a Bible study together. They are not experiencing what it means to be on mission together in the everyday stuff of life. So they live with the facade that everything is OK. On the surface, they look as if they are all in for Jesus. But brokenness, pride, insecurity, and selfishness are all there under the surface.

The Mission Trip Never Ends

Are you on mission with others, together discovering your desperate need for God's power and grace?

If not, you are not likely to grow up much toward maturity, and you are likely living with little experience of the presence and power of God's Spirit because the life you're living doesn't really require God's Spirit.

Some of the members of our church just returned from spending time with some members of the persecuted church. They remarked about how filled with faith these people are as they seek to share the gospel every day with unbelievers. They said that people pray with fervency and read their Bibles consistently because they have to do so in order to persevere in the daily task of being on Jesus's mission, especially knowing they will suffer for their faith for the sake of Jesus.

We have much to learn from the persecuted church that is on mission every moment.

We don't have to wait until persecution comes, however. We need to get on mission now, together, every day.

And let's make sure the mission trip never ends—at least until Jesus returns to finish the work.

Life on mission is where:

- our brokenness and ongoing need for God's help is exposed,
- training for making disciples occurs, and
- the power of the Spirit is displayed.

Life on mission is not just about *being* disciples, but also about *making* disciples who make disciples—and that can be learned only while on Jesus's mission.

Part 4

New Identity

You Do Who You Are

"We have an identity problem," I said to my friend Caesar.

We were meeting in our makeshift offices, which had been jumbled together out of some portable dividers in a warehouse that had previously been part of a company that made fleece-ware for Eddie Bauer. We had been working hard to lead our people to love one another well and remain on the mission of making disciples together. Caesar and Tina had moved to join our team about a year into our beginning, and they were good examples of people who opened their homes and engaged regularly with people who didn't yet know the love of Jesus.

Our people seemed to be doing well at loving one another, but they were having a hard time regularly engaging in the lives of the people in our city. It seemed we had to remind them of what to do on a weekly basis. Unfortunately, it also seemed as if we had adopted a new kind of legalism—a "missional to-do list"—that left the members feeling like spiritual slaves and left the leaders feeling like taskmasters. This was clearly not the free and abundant life the gospel promised to deliver.

Have you ever experienced this—Christianity as a new set of rules or tasks? Maybe you've even begun to engage in mission outside of church events, only to find that you've just adopted a new form of slavery to a big missional to-do list.

The gospel offers us something far better than a missional to-do list.

At this time, I was doing a personal study through Paul's letters, and something I'd seen before stood out to me in a different way. Whenever the people in the churches that Paul influenced went sideways, Paul didn't just confront their wrongdoing and tell them what to do. He started by reminding them of who God is, what he had done for them in Jesus, and who they were in light of that. Then he reminded them of how believing the truth about the gospel and their new identity would lead them to a different behavior. Paul knew that all of our behaviors are the result of what we believe about *who God is* as revealed through *what God does*, leading to what we believe about *who we are*. God's work in Jesus Christ grants us a whole new identity, and this new identity leads to a whole new way of living.

We do what we do because of who we are.

You do who you are. Being precedes doing.

God is and God does. And he does who he is. His activity reveals the truth about who he is.

Think about how backward the world is on this. The world defines people based upon what they do, not who they are.

What generally happens when you meet someone for the first time? "Hello, my name is Bill," you say. Then the other person says, "Nice to meet you, Bill." What generally comes next?

"So . . . what do you do?"

You reply that you're a teacher, a plumber, a doctor, a

barista, a banker, or any number of other possible professions. We define people—even ourselves—by what they do, not by who they are.

Has anyone ever asked you, after hearing your name, "Who are you?" I've done this. It startles people, because they don't tend to know who they are apart from what they do. But we're not human *doings*. We're human *beings*.

Think about how unstable you are when you define yourself by what you do. What happens when you can't do it anymore? Or imagine you're just no good at what you do. In the first case, your identity is taken away. In the second case, your identity is "Failure" or "Incompetent."

One of our neighbors was a longtime teacher who was very good at what he did. One day, however, he informed me that he had lost his job. He asked if we could get together for lunch and talk about it. Over a plate of Mexican food, I asked him how he was doing. He said: "Not well. It's not losing a paycheck that's so hard for me. We've got enough in the bank to cover our financial needs. The real problem, I'm discovering, is that my job was my identity. I'm not really sure who I am anymore. And what's even worse is that while I could get another teaching position, I'm now aware that it's not stable. I could lose it again. My identity can come and go that quickly, over and over again."

This is a real problem.

What's your identity? Do you know who you are? Or have you looked to something or someone for significance, only to find that that thing or person ended up defining you?

If you're going to school, you'd probably say you're a student. But what about when you graduate? Graduating would not be altogether devastating—unless you can't get a job. Who would you be then?

Or maybe you'd describe yourself as a mom. But what about

when your children move away or, worse, what if they are taken from you early in life through an accident or sickness? Your children would be gone. Who would you be then?

What if you defined yourself as a husband, but your wife left you? Who would you be?

These things happen. We lose our jobs, our places in life, and our relationships. And if they define who we are, we also lose our identity.

Who are you when all that you can do, produce, or manage is gone? Most of us don't know, so we keep doing more to gain some sense of identity.

The Failure of Adam and Eve

Where does this problem come from? It began in the garden with Adam and Eve.

Remember the beginning? God created man and woman in his image—in his likeness—and, after creating them and the world they lived in, he said, "This is very good!" This was another way of saying, "This is right—this is righteous!" Humans were a visible representation of what God is like. And God was absolutely satisfied with his work—it rightly expressed the truth about him. God told Adam and Eve to believe his word and to trust in his work. Their expression of that trust would be to do what he created them to do—perform good work, start a family that would lead to more families, and rule the world well. They were to do what they did out of faith in who God is and what he had done.

God is the Creator (*who he is*) who created (*what he did*) images of himself (*who we are*) to create and co-create (*what we do*).

Do you see the progression?

Who God is (Creator)

is revealed through what God has done (created),
which leads to who we are (image bearers created in God's likeness)
and what we do (display God and co-create more image bearers).

First, we come to know what God is like by what he does. That is how he reveals his identity to us. And what he does to us makes us who we are, because, as God, he made us and defines us. He created us, and therefore his work defines who we are. Then, whenever God does something to you, he also intends to do something through you. Our work in the world is an extension *and* expression of God's very identity.

God is ruler: he rules, and he gave humanity power to rule so that we might rule over the earth.

God is lover: he loves us through Jesus so that we might love one another.

God is judge: he judges us and justifies us in Jesus so that we might exercise justice.

Do you see how God works in and through us? This is how God intends to fill the world with the knowledge of his glory through his image bearers.

We only need to believe, that is, to trust in (1) what God has revealed about himself (his Word), (2) what he has done (his work), and (3) who he has made us to be (his workmanship). If we believe in his Word and work, we will do what God would have us do (our work).

This is how it always works. Everything you or I do comes out of what we believe about God, God's Word, and God's work. Our behaviors reveal what we believe about these things.

God also told Adam and Eve to show their faith in him by *not doing* something: "Of the tree of the knowledge of good and evil you shall not eat, for in the day that you eat of it you shall surely die" (Gen. 2:17).

This seems pretty simple, doesn't it? Everything was great. There was delicious food all around, the entire created world was in submission to humanity, and man and woman were perfectly united in love. And the only restriction was going elsewhere for the definition of what made them good.

God was saying: "Trust me. Believe my word and show you believe by obeying me—don't go outside of me and my word to find your significance."

One day, the evil Tempter came into the garden and began to question Eve:

> "Did God actually say, 'You shall not eat of any tree in the garden'?" And the woman said to the serpent, "We may eat of the fruit of the trees in the garden, but God said, 'You shall not eat of the fruit of the tree that is in the midst of the garden, neither shall you touch it, lest you die.'" But the serpent said to the woman, "You will not surely die. For God knows that when you eat of it your eyes will be opened, and you will be like God, knowing good and evil." (Gen. 3:1–5)

Notice what the Tempter did. He questioned God's word—"You will not surely die"—and he questioned God's work—"You will be like God."

In essence, he was saying, "God is a liar and God's work was insufficient."

And he promised that through their work (eating the fruit) they could *become like God*. This was the origin of our tendency to find our identity outside of God and in our own works.

But they already were like God!

Do you see what the Tempter was saying? "Don't look to God to define you, to declare you good! Look elsewhere. Look to what *I* say will make you great. Look to *yourself*. Look to *what you do*!"

Pause here for a moment.

Who or what is defining you? Are you letting someone or

something other than God's Word and work define you? Are you defining yourself? Are you looking to your own abilities and actions to make you who you are? Are you looking to what has been done to you or what you hope will be done to you to define you?

Eve was deceived. She believed the Serpent and saw the tree as something to be desired to make one wise. Wisdom in the Bible offers everyday direction for how to live the best life possible, but Eve saw the Deceiver, the tree, and herself as more effective than God at this point. She exchanged the Creator for creation as the guide for wisdom. She ate the fruit and gave some to her husband, who also ate. Then their eyes were opened and they realized they were naked. They sewed fig leaves together and made coverings for themselves.

Adam and Eve had been created in God's likeness, but instead of trusting in God's word and work, they trusted in another's word and in their own works to give them their identity. The result, however, was not better, but worse. The Tempter's words were a lie, the opposite of the truth of God. Their own works were nothing compared to God's work.

So in their rebellious unbelief, they felt shame and inadequacy. Next, they covered themselves with more of their own work, sewing fig leaves together to make loincloths. This wasn't sufficient, so they hid from the Lord when he came walking through the garden.

This rebellion shattered their identity and tore apart their relationships with God, each other, and the created world in which they lived. And it didn't end with them. Their rebelliousness was passed on from generation to generation. To this day, people are working for an identity, trying to cover up their shame with more hard work, and then hiding when their work doesn't measure up or cover them adequately.

I've done it. You've done it. And we continue to do it.

What are you trying to cover your life with? What kinds of things are you doing in an effort to hide your sense of inadequacy or shame? What are your "fig leaves"—the works you are trusting instead of God's Word and work?

The Faithfulness of Abram

Thankfully, God was not fine with leaving the human race in this state. He had a plan all along. Eventually, God called another man, Abram, and promised to bless him, make him a great nation, and make his name great so that through him God could bless all peoples on the earth (Gen. 12:1–3). He and his wife, Sarai, were old and incapable of having children, but God promised that their offspring would be as numerous as the stars in the heavens. Abram believed God, and for that, God considered him righteous (Gen. 15:6). He did what Adam and Eve did not—he believed in God's word and God's work regarding his identity.

Eventually, God changed Abram's name to Abraham, which means "father of a multitude," saying, "I have made you the father of a multitude of nations" (Gen. 17:5). I love how God called Abraham something before anything had been done!

Can you imagine what Abraham must have been thinking? "God just said I am the father of a multitude of nations. I have no children. We can't have children. God says something is true of me even before I do something about it—even though I *can't* do anything about it! Is this how it works with God? Wow! This is amazing!"

This is how God works! He says something is and it is. This is how he created the world. He spoke and it came into existence. With Abraham, he was forming a people. He spoke and they came into existence.

This is what he does in us as well. He doesn't ask you to make yourself into somebody. *He* makes you into somebody.

He speaks over your life through Jesus, the Word made flesh, the better Word and the better work of God. And *he* makes you new. He gives you a new identity with a new name.

Jesus was born into the genealogical line of Abraham. In him, God's ultimate blessing came to earth. Jesus is the perfect Word and perfect work of God. The Father once again said, "This is very good!," this time over his own Son. Jesus is the righteousness of God. And all who believe in him as God's perfect Word and work for us are counted righteous. God says over you, "You are very good!"

After Jesus died and rose again, just before he ascended back to the right hand of the Father, he commissioned his disciples, saying: "All authority in heaven and on earth has been given to me. Go therefore and make disciples of all nations, baptizing them *in the name* of the Father and of the Son and of the Holy Spirit, teaching them to observe all that I have commanded you. And behold, I am with you always, to the end of the age" (Matt. 28:18–20).

Jesus had claimed back the authority that Adam and Eve had given away, and he was bringing about a new beginning—a new creation. This new creation has a new people—people who were dead in their sins and defined by the works of sinful humanity, but who are now alive in Christ and defined by Jesus, the better Word and the better work. Paul says to the church in Corinth: "Therefore, if anyone is in Christ, he is a new creation. The old has passed away; behold, the new has come" (2 Cor. 5:17).

Our new-creation identity is expressed in our baptism. To baptize is to saturate. Our baptism represents that we are now saturated within the Godhead. This saturation into God makes us different. God changes us. This is very important, because God wants us to know that we are new creations with new identities in him before he calls us to live new lives.

This is why Jesus commands that we baptize disciples *in the name* of the Father, the Son, and the Holy Spirit. Our baptism is a physical display of our old life of sin and death being buried with Jesus Christ in his death. It is also a sign of our new life of faith, hope, and love, as we have been raised with Christ into new life. We have a new life, a new identity, and a new name. Just as Abram was given a new name that represented what God had done and would do through him, our new name represents what God has done and will do through us.

Whatever God does to you, he also plans to do through you.

In order to effectively live out the purposes of God for our lives together on mission, we need to know and believe our new identity, because it is out of this that we will do everything we do.

Do you know who you are in Christ? Do you know your new name?

If your faith is in Jesus Christ, your life is in him. You are baptized into the *name* of the Father, the Son, and the Holy Spirit. This means:

1. God is our Father and we are his family.
2. Jesus is our Lord and we are his servants.
3. The Holy Spirit is our Guide and Sender, and we are his missionaries.

Your new name represents both who God says you are and what he plans to do through you. You are saturated with the Father, the Son, and the Holy Spirit. It starts with God and his work, which changes you so new work can come through you.

If the world is going to experience gospel saturation through Jesus's people, we must first be saturated with the Father, the Son, and the Holy Spirit. Then, what God does to us he will also do through us.

We Are Family: Baptized into the Name of the Father

"I wash my hands of that woman!" Jayne said in exasperation. She was fed up with Nicki, our neighbor. Nicki regularly used her van to nudge her garbage cans forward into the parking space in front of our home. Jayne moved them back, over and over again. "That's it!" Jayne thought as she picked up the cans and put them right in the middle of Nicki's yard. "I'm done with her; she is impossible!" As far as Jayne was concerned, there would be no more attempts to reach Nicki.

When we moved into our home in Tacoma, Nicki didn't introduce herself to us; instead, the neighbors told us about her. "We're sorry about that eyesore next to you," they said. Nicki's house was falling apart. The bushes were overgrown, invading every crack and crevice. The front yard was full of weeds, and the backyard was a jungle with blackberry bushes growing as high as twenty feet, covering two broken-down cars and a rotting deck. It was a perfect home for the urban animals that often climbed her fence into our backyard.

Others in the neighborhood had tried to help her, but they had given up as well. It's not easy reaching out to someone whose face is turned downward or away every time you extend a welcome. Like the neighbors, we found this out firsthand. No matter how many times we tried to reach out to Nicki, she rejected our attempts. She was a hurting woman, and she made it clear she didn't want us in her life.

Nicki had been married at a very young age to a very difficult man. She never really felt loved by him. Eventually, they divorced and she remarried. Her second husband, Bud, was Nicki's angel—at least that's how she described him to us. According to her, they had a wonderful marriage. Then he died of cancer. Nicki had opened her life to someone and had felt loved, but then he was gone. She didn't want to go through that again: open up and receive love, only to lose it.

So she isolated herself. She became a hoarder. She closed herself up in her house, slowly dying inside. She needed love, but she didn't want to risk losing love.

Shortly after Jayne gave up, Nicki showed up at our front door. She was in tears. A taxi had just dropped her off because her van had broken down and needed to be towed to a repair shop. This was the first time that Jayne had ever had a close face-to-face conversation with Nicki. "I'm so sorry to bother you," Nicki said, "but you've always been so friendly. I didn't know where to go, and I need some help." What followed was a three-hour conversation, in which Nicki began to pour her heart out to Jayne, and Jayne began to feel a deep empathy for Nicki.

Jayne had given up on Nicki, but God had moved her toward us. He loved her more than we ever could. We had perceived Nicki as a project. But it's not our job to change people. That's God's job. He sends us to love people so that they can come to know the Father's love through us. I'll never forget when I sensed the Spirit saying, "Love Nicki like she is part of the family."

That's what Jesus did with us. That's what he wants to do through us. Whatever he has done to you, he now wants to do through you.

Loving as Jesus Loves

Jesus said: "A new commandment I give you, that you love one another: just as I have loved you, you also are to love one another. By this all people will know that you are my disciples, if you have love for one another" (John 13:34–35).

Without Jesus, we were dead in our sins and by nature children of wrath. We were enemies of God because of our sinful rebellion against him. There was a time when we couldn't come to God with personal knowledge of his love and acceptance of us. But God is full of mercy, and he changed everything for us through Jesus (Eph. 2:1–6). God showed his love for us in that while we were enemies, he gave his Son to die for us, to make us his dearly loved children (Rom. 5:8; 8:14–17). We have been adopted into God's family so that we are now coheirs with Jesus Christ. We have been born again by his Spirit, making us the true children of God (John 1:12–13; 3:3–8).

If your life is now hidden with Christ Jesus (Col. 3:3), God dearly loves you, regardless of what you've done or will do. Just as God the Father loves the Son, so he loves you. Just as the Father said of Jesus the Son, "This is my beloved Son, with whom I am well pleased" (Matt. 3:17), he now says the same over you.

Do you believe this? Do you believe in God's Word and

work regarding you and your standing in the family of God? Do you believe you are dearly loved regardless of your work, good or bad?

You are a child of God, part of his family. This is your new identity, for you have been baptized in the name of the Father. As a result, you have a new name: *Child of the Father. Son of God. Daughter of God*

If you believe this to be true, it changes how you live and how you love.

What God has done to you, he now wants to do through you.

In the previous chapter, we considered who God is and what he has done, as well as who we are and what we are to do. Let's think through those categories again in light of our baptism in the name of the Father. Consider these four questions: *Who is God?* He is our Father. *What has he done?* He has loved us by sending his Son, Jesus, to die for our sins. *Who are we?* We are the dearly loved children of God—God's family. If we believe this, *what do we do?* We love one another as brothers and sisters in the same way God has loved us.

God has perfectly loved you so that, through you, he might love others. He pours his perfect love into your heart through his Spirit in order that you might love others with the love he gives you. When you believe the gospel regarding God's love for you, you love others because he loved you first. If you believe God dearly loves you, you will love others in the same ways he loves you.

You will love others like family.

So we asked ourselves, "If Nicki were our mother, sister, or daughter, how would we love her?" That simple question changed everything for us—and our missional community.

One question led to others: "If we were to see Nicki as our mother, sister, or daughter, how patient would we be with her?

Would we give up on her? What kinds of things might we do for her? How would we express love for her? If that love looked like God's love for us, what would we do?"

Together, we started loving her like family: like a mother, a sister, or a daughter of our heavenly Father.

Nicki came to our door again. She was in terrible condition and needed to get to the hospital. However, her van was still broken down and she was unwilling to call an ambulance because she didn't want the neighborhood to know she was in need.

Nicki was isolated, hiding, shamed, and broken. But she was not alone. God had put us there because he loved her, so he was present for her through us. We were Jesus's body in Nicki's life to love her toward Jesus.

She had been growing to trust us, though she hadn't always responded well to our love. She had continued to keep us at a distance, but she could see we hadn't given up on her. We had continued to tell her we were there and we were not going away. That's what a family does. It doesn't give up.

Jesus doesn't give up on us either.

He's not wearied by our ongoing brokenness. He's not repelled by our insecurities and fears, which lead us to run away into isolation. He is present. He is here. He is not leaving. Because he loves us like family, even when we don't treat him like a brother or look to God as our Father, he never changes and he doesn't give up.

That's how we could love Nicki like family. We were loving her with the love we had received from God the Father through Jesus.

So Jayne took her to the hospital. Nicki had to stay for several days, so we visited her. People brought her flowers and prayed with her at her bedside. We loved her like she was part of our family.

When she returned home, we asked about her van. At our

next family gathering over dinner, someone suggested we pay to have Nicki's van fixed. Later that week, we offered. She accepted, but it took several months for her to finally give us the keys. In the meantime, we let her use our vehicles to get around town. This kind of familial love for Nicki continued. We fixed broken windows in her house, paid her utility bill when she couldn't, had her over for meals, invited her to join us for Thanksgiving and Christmas, and threw her a birthday party.

It was costly. It felt intrusive. We didn't always feel up to it. It even required some hard conversations with our immediate family as we started including her more and more in our celebrations.

Eventually, after numerous conversations, Nicki came to believe God really loved her. I'll never forget the day when she came over to tell Jayne that she had surrendered her life to Jesus and experienced his grace to forgive her of her sins. Jayne asked her who Jesus was to her now. "He's my Father," Nicki responded. When Jayne shared this, I remember thinking: "Oh, no! We didn't teach her about the Trinity! We've got to teach her about God the Father, God the Son, and God the Spirit." Then the Spirit of God reminded me: "Remember what Jesus said: 'Whoever has seen me has seen the Father' (John 14:9). Nicki has it right. What she needed most was to know the love of the Father for her, and she now knows the Father's love through Jesus."

Nicki came to know the Father's love through Jesus the Son, expressed both at the cross and through his body, the church, living next door to her and loving her like family.

Love Builds the Family

Nicki didn't experience a total life change. She was a work in progress—slower than I'd prefer, to be honest. That is what discipleship is—a process. She still had a lot of brokenness; many areas of her life needed restoration. Yet she was part of God's family, loved and accepted nonetheless. Over time, we watched the love of the Father start to flow outward from her to others as well. Nicki became a grandmother to all of our children and like a mother to many of the adults in the group. We all grew to love Nicki very much over the next several years.

In the summer of 2014, while our family was on vacation, we received a phone call that Nicki had suffered cardiac arrest while driving her car. She subsequently had crashed into a tree. The paramedics revived her, but she arrested two more times on the way to the hospital. They had to put her on life support. Some dear friends of ours picked Jayne up and drove her to the hospital, which was more than three hours from where we were staying. Our whole missional community took shifts being with Nicki throughout the day and night.

During the next couple of days, our group met Nicki's estranged daughter and grandson. Our group showed them the same love we had showed Nicki. They were overwhelmed with disbelief. They must have been wondering, "Who loves like this?" God the Father does, through people like us. We loved them like family.

On August 14, 2014, the doctors disconnected Nicki from the breathing machine. She passed away a little while later.

Grandma Nicki died, but not alone. She had a family, a forever family.

We loved and we lost this time—at least temporarily.

Now Nicki is united to the man of her dreams. Sure, Bud, is there in heaven. But that's not the man I'm talking about. Nicki went to be with Jesus!

She is with the love of her life because God used us to introduce her to his love through us.

It hasn't stopped there. Recently, Nicki's grandson Jonathan joined our missional community. He started to become part of the family. We have been helping him clean out and restore Nicki's house, and he decided he wants to move in next door and join the family! Lately, he's been hanging out for meals and staying late for many conversations about Jesus.

One night, he asked me to explain baptism to him. After I described what it means and why we do it, he said, "Well, I'm a little nervous asking you this, but could I get baptized in the ocean this weekend during our retreat?" So we baptized Jonathan in the Pacific Ocean. The story is still being written, and the family is only getting bigger!

Think about where you live. Do you know your neighbors? Has God given you a heart to love them like family? What would it look like if you did?

What about the people in your small group or missional community? Do you love one another this way? How might your group change if you did?

Now think about who God has sent you to (your neighbors, coworkers, peers at school, and others). What might it look like if you were to love them as if they were your brothers and sisters? Like children of our Father in heaven?

"But they're not," you might say. "They don't yet belong to God."

Yes, but we don't know whom he is drawing to himself. And how will they ever come to know the love of God the Father if they don't experience it through us? Consider those God has put around you as the lost children of God who don't yet know how much their Father loves them. Then show them his Fatherly love in tangible ways.

"But, you don't get it!" you might say. "The people around me are jerks!"

So were you to God. Remember, you were an enemy of God, and he loved you like his own child, dearly beloved, through Jesus.

"Yes, but I don't want to be a doormat!" you might say.

"I serve, and they never seem grateful. Some just keep taking advantage of me."

I know—just like we do with our heavenly Father's love.

We have yet to fully express the gratitude God deserves for giving us his Son and continuing to be gracious to us. Besides, if anyone was treated like a doormat, it was Jesus while he was hanging on a cross, dying for the sins of humanity while they spat on him and mocked him.

We love because we were first loved. And we love with the same love with which he loved us.

When we fail to love, we show we don't yet fully know the love of God for us. We don't know who God is, what he has done, and who we are in Christ.

We need the Spirit of God to continue to reveal these truths to our hearts, to pour the love of God the Father into our hearts that we might love others with the same love and in the same way he has loved us.

Baptized into the name of the Father, we are his family so that we might love one another as he has loved us.

If you want to see the world around you saturated with the good news of Jesus, it will start with you and others loving one another as family and loving those around you like the lost children of God whom he is wooing back to himself through his love poured out through you.

We Are Servants: Baptized into the Name of the Son (the King)

In the beginning, God gave Adam and Eve rule and reign over all the earth. God made them in his image to be a constant reminder to the entire created world that he is the ultimate ruler over all. Everywhere they went, they were to represent God's rule and reign in all they did. Then, as they had children, who likewise would be image bearers, those children also would be a visible reminder of God's rule and reign. This is why Adam and Eve were to be fruitful, multiply, and fill the earth. God's intent was to fill the earth with his image—his glory on display—so that all of creation would show what he is like. That's saturation.

Who is God? The Ruler. *What has he done?* He has created vice-regents to submit to his rule and to reign over all of creation. *Who are we?* We are vice-regents given dominion over the earth. *What do we do?* We rule on God's behalf like he would.

However, the Evil One tricked Adam and Eve into submitting to him as the ruler of the world instead of God. In that moment, they handed over their authority to Satan, and in exchange, they became his slaves. The father of sin and lies became the god of this world. And all of humanity, from that point on, was born into this reality—slavery to sin and to Satan, the god of this world.

It is very apparent that his rule is rotten. Everything is broken under his authority. Relationships are divided and broken. Families are broken, leaving the fatherless and the widow without families. Hatred toward one another is expressed through slander, gossip, and even murder. Selfishness corrupts everything, leading to greed, poverty, and all kinds of abuse and injustice. And the beautiful world God created for us to enjoy and rule continues to be destroyed through human depravity.

So Jesus came as the new human King we all need. He came to set the captives free and bring about a new kingdom where everything would be restored to its previous place under God's very good rule. Jesus is the new King, the new Adam, sent to establish God's rule and reign over all the earth.

Jesus didn't come like other kings do. The reigns of all other kings more resemble the rule and reign of Adam, with people enslaved to sin, than the rule and reign of God, where people are free to obey and live life to the full. And all other kings come not to serve but be served. They need what others have and what others can do. They need authority, so they grasp for it, taking it by force, just as Satan did. The kings of this world need land, so they go to war. They need armies to fight to get the land, but armies come at a cost. So they need money. They need to persuade some of the rich to fund their wars. To do this, they need wise counselors to convince the wealthy that the kings know what they're talking about. So the kings need wise people around them. The kings of this world are in need. They need authority, land, armies, money, wise counselors, and much more.

On the other hand, there's Jesus the King. Consider how he arrived. He came humbly. God became human in the form of a baby. Paul reminded the Philippian church that although Jesus was in very nature God, he "did not count equality with God a thing to be grasped, but emptied himself, by taking the form of a servant, being born in the likeness of men. . . . He humbled himself by becoming obedient to the point of death, even death on a cross. Therefore God has highly exalted him and bestowed on him the name that is above every name" (Phil. 2:6–9). Jesus refused to grasp for the authority that was rightly his so that we, who continue to wrongly grasp for authority that is not rightly ours, might be forgiven. Jesus humbled himself, taking on the form of a servant, so that we, who have become slaves to sin through our rebellious pride, might be set free to serve God once again. And Jesus, who was rich, became poor, so that in his poverty, we might become rich (2 Cor. 8:9). Under Jesus's rule and reign, the kingdom belongs to the poor in spirit, and the meek inherit the earth (Matt. 5:3, 5). Those who lack have their needs met. The least in the kingdom become the greatest.

Jesus came as a King, but his posture is that of a servant. He did not come to be served, for he needed nothing. He came to serve, because we needed everything he had! And he provided us with everything we need as a servant who laid down his life so we could have life.

If you have come to Jesus the Servant of all—the King of all kings—you did so because you knew you needed him to serve you. You knew you needed him to rescue you from your slavery to sin and Satan, to heal you from your spiritual sickness, to fill your spiritual poverty with his incredible riches, and to cover your sinful nakedness and shame with his clothing of righteousness. If this is true of you, you have been delivered from the kingdom of darkness under Satan's rule and authority, and transferred to the kingdom of light under the rule and reign of Jesus (Col. 1:13).

This means you are no longer a slave to sin but a servant of righteousness. You are no longer a servant in the kingdom of darkness, but a servant to the King of righteousness (Rom. 6:15–23). Jesus is your King, and you are his servant. And whatever you do to others, you are now doing unto Jesus your King. When you serve others, you are serving him, because this is the nature of his kingdom (Matt. 25:31–46).

Baptized into the name of the Father, we are his dearly loved children, who love one another like family.

Baptized into the name of the Son, we are set free to be servants of Jesus, who give tangible expression to the love of God through serving others.

Jesus is the embodiment of the Father's love for us. Now, we, his people, are the body of Christ, who express God's love for others through our acts of service.

What God has done to you, he now wants to do through you.

Pointing toward the Kingdom

Think through our four questions again.

Who is God? He is our King (the Son). *What has he done?* He came not to be served, but to serve, and to give his life as a ransom for many. *Who are we?* We are servants of the King of kings. If we believe this, *what do we do?* We serve the least of the people of the world as an act of worship of our King.

This is what it means to be the *soma* ("body") of Jesus.

Through our lives, Jesus is showing the world the kind of King he is and the nature of the kingdom he rules. As his servants, we point forward with our acts of service to a far better world where Jesus's rule will be experienced everywhere. Everyone we serve experiences a taste of life in the kingdom.

So where in our world are people *not* getting to experience the life of Jesus's kingdom? And what would that life look like if Jesus brought about his rule and reign through us? What would we do if we believed we really are his servants and he really is ruling?

The members of one of our missional communities began to believe their new identity as servants and started to live it out in a very tangible way. They lived in a part of our city that was largely made up of homes led by single moms. In most cases, these moms were working two or three jobs, but still barely getting by. The missional community discovered that most of the kids in the neighborhood didn't get to have birthday parties. Some had never had one. The families just couldn't afford parties. So the members of the community determined to ensure that every child in their neighborhood had a birthday party that year.

In the kingdom of God, everyone belongs to the family and every life is celebrated. Every child gets a party.

I was so encouraged when I heard about one of the parties. A little boy, with no father present, was surrounded by men and women singing "Happy Birthday" to him. When he saw the cake, he said, "What is that?" He was told, "It's your birthday cake." Amazed, he asked, "It's mine?" and when he was assured that it was, he said, "Wow!" Next, one of our members invited people to speak words of blessing and encouragement over this boy. One by one, people verbally blessed him. When it came time for him to open the mountain of presents, he again asked what they were and had to be assured they were his.

Again he said, "Wow!" While all this was happening, his mom was sitting back with tears streaming down her face. She never could have given her son this party. But Jesus's servants could.

Jesus's servants look around and see where things are not as they ought to be. They know what things should be like because they know the story of God's rule and reign in the first garden and the promise of his rule and reign in the future, gardenlike city. When Jesus is King over all and everything is in submission to him, there will be no more sin—no more brokenness, no more sickness, no more pain—and we will all have a Father and brothers and sisters. We will all have plenty, and no one will go without. Children will get to have parties. And Jesus will be at the center of it all.

I recently took my son Caleb on a father-and-son retreat with several other fathers and sons from Soma. There also were a few single men and some married men who don't have sons. Greg, our poker party friend, who now helps families transition out of homelessness, had connected some boys from the families he works with to some of our men who have no children or have only daughters. For instance, Jonathan, a single man, was there with Jessica's son, Holden. Jessica is a single mom, and Jonathan is one of the leaders of her missional community. Jonathan stepped into the role of father for the weekend so Holden could join us. I was blessed to see all of these men leading and loving these boys as if they were their own children.

In Jesus's kingdom, the fatherless get fathered.

I've observed our men do this through coaching sports and bringing boys along. Others lead sandlot summer baseball training weeks in local parks and invite all the families who might not be able to afford Little League. Moms invite other children to join them for playdates when some single moms need a break. Jayne does hospice work in order to care for the dying, many of whom have no one with them in their final days. Students struggling in school get after-school mentoring. Properties once used for drug dealing and prostitution have been turned into community gardens. Broken-down houses and fences have been repaired. AIDS hospice homes have been maintained. Buildings tagged by graffiti have been painted.

Everywhere Jesus's people are engaged like this, they serve their King and represent his kingdom.

Look around you. Consider where God has placed you and others with you. Does it look like Jesus's kingdom? Are the hungry fed, the naked clothed, the broken brought to health, the disconnected included in families, and the captives set free to fully live? If we are servants of Jesus, we are in the place where he has put us in order to serve others as he served us. He wants people to experience what life can be like in his kingdom through his body, the church. As his body, we give tangible expression to what Jesus is like. He wants people to taste and see, through our actions of love, that he is very good and his kingdom is amazing, so that, after experiencing it, they will want to be with him forever in his kingdom.

Worshiping through Our Work

Recently, a couple of members of our church, Mark and Coby, two businessmen who have started their own companies, taught the rest of us that believing our identity as servants is absolutely core to how we look at our work as well. We spend more than one-third of our lives working at our jobs. Many of us go to work thinking we are primarily working for a paycheck, a promotion, or a sense of success or significance. If those are the reasons we work, we end up forgetting our identity as servants of the King for one-third of our lives. In so doing, we slip right back into slavery, and we fail to worship our King fully at work. When this happens, we also miss out on the opportunity to show our coworkers what our King is like through how we serve him.

If there is any place that needs to experience the change that Jesus's kingdom brings, it is the workplace.

Paul commands us to go to work for our King: "Whatever you do, work heartily, as for the Lord and not for men" (Col. 3:23).

What if we started believing that Jesus is our true and better boss? What if we went to work all day for him?

He's already paid us far better than we deserve: "The wages of sin is death, but the gift of God is eternal life in Jesus Christ our Lord" (Rom. 6:23). Eternal life—what a paycheck!

He has already promoted us to the highest place: God "raised us up with him and seated us with him in the heavenly places in Christ Jesus" (Eph. 2:6).

We are loved, though we have performed poorly. We are accepted by God when we should be rejected. We have an amazing boss who is always just, always has our best interests in mind, and guarantees us the best "retirement" package there is.

Go to work for that boss!

Then see your work as a means of worshiping Jesus. That is what he calls real worship anyway—serving him with our very bodies (Rom. 12:1).

God intends to saturate not just our leisure hours and weekends with the good news of Jesus. He also intends to saturate our work hours by leading us to serve and worship him while we work. Can you imagine what it would look like if you saw every workday as a worship service? How would you work differently? How would you care for your fellow employees? What if, like Jesus, you and I were more committed to the welfare of others than to our own promotions?

As we serve others as Jesus served us, and work unto the Lord at our workplaces, we bring the experience of Jesus's kingdom into the world. That's what his servants do in their homes, neighborhoods, workplaces, and cities. We do it all so people can experience the greatness of our Servant King and come to him in order to be set free to serve him with all of their hearts and lives as well.

Baptized into the name of the Son, we are his servants. Therefore, we serve the least of the people of the world just as he served us.

$$14$$

We Are Missionaries: Baptized into the Name of the Holy Spirit

"I don't know how God could ever work through me like he does through you, Jeff!" Clay said. I had just informed him that he also would experience God working through him by his Spirit to share the gospel as one of God's missionaries. He had recently come to faith and clearly had received God's Spirit. I wanted him to know that he was now going to be sent by God just as I was—just as Jesus was.

God dwells with his people, and they are missionaries whom he sends into the everyday stuff of life. Jesus intends to saturate the world with his presence through his Sprit in his people—his sent ones.

God dwelt with Adam and Eve in the garden and gave them a mission to accomplish with his presence and help. But when they rebelled against him, he drove them out.

He dwelt with his people Israel while they traveled in the desert. Moses told God he would not go to the Promised Land unless God went with them. He asked God: "How shall it be known that I have found favor in your sight, I and your people? Is it not in your going with us, so that we are distinct, I and your people, from every other people on the face of the earth?" (Ex. 33:16). Moses knew that it was God with them that gave them their identity, purpose, and power. Eventually, God instructed his people to build him a dwelling place (the tabernacle), where he would dwell with them when they paused in their travels. When they finally arrived in the land, they eventually built a temple as a permanent place of dwelling for the Lord. Before God came to dwell in the tabernacle and temple, both had to be purified by the shedding of the blood of an innocent animal. Once the tabernacle or temple and its articles of worship were purified, God dwelt there.

However, a better dwelling place was to come. God wanted to dwell not only *with* his people. He wanted to dwell *in* his people.

So he sent the Son—Jesus.

Jesus was conceived by the Holy Spirit and born of the Virgin Mary. God's Son became flesh and dwelt among us. God set up his tabernacle—his temple—in the person of Jesus.

Now *we* become children of God through regeneration brought about by the same Holy Spirit. We are born again of the Spirit (John 3:3–9). When this happens, we are new creations with a new spiritual DNA. Christ, the very life of God, is in us. If we belong to Christ, we have the Spirit of Christ (Rom. 8:9–11). The presence of God's Spirit in our lives is the evidence that our lives have been cleansed by the blood of Jesus shed on the cross for our sins. Just as God dwelt in the tabernacle and the temple after they had been cleansed, he now dwells in us, who by faith have been cleansed by the blood of Jesus.

We are the temple of the living God! God is present and living in us by his Spirit.

Jesus was baptized by John in the Jordan River before he began his earthly ministry. When he came out of the waters of baptism, the Spirit descended upon him in the form of a dove and the Father said, "This is my beloved Son, with whom I am well pleased" (Matt. 3:17). Jesus was assured of the Father's love before he went out to love others.

The same is now true for us. We need the same affirmation. If we are going to show the world the love of the Father, we need to know we are dearly loved by him as well!

Jesus said, "As the Father has sent me, even so I am sending you" (John 20:21). We are sent like Jesus, with the presence and power of the Spirit reminding us of the love of the Father.

We need the constant reminder that we are God's dearly loved children. God gives us his Spirit to remind us that he is our true Father and he loves us very much.

Strength against Temptation

But it doesn't end there. Jesus was not just accompanied by the Holy Spirit. He also was filled with and led by the Holy Spirit to be tempted by the Devil. Just as Adam and Eve were tempted, so Jesus also had to be tempted in order to accomplish what Adam and Eve could not.

Jesus was tempted by the Devil, but he did not give in (Luke 4:1–13).

How did Jesus overcome the temptations? So many Christians who are familiar with this passage answer, "He quoted the Bible." Yes, he did. But so did the Devil. Just knowing and speaking the Bible alone does not enable one to overcome temptation.

Jesus knew the Bible. He quoted the Scriptures. And he was led and filled by the Holy Spirit. The same Spirit that inspired the Scriptures helped Jesus to obey them and resist temptation.

The same is true for us.

"As the Father has sent me, even so I am sending you."

He sends us with the Spirit's power to know and understand God's Word, to obey it, and to resist the temptation to disobey it.

We were attending a Kings of Leon concert at the Gorge, an outdoor concert amphitheater on the Columbia River. We camped out with our group; some of them knew and loved Jesus, while others had not yet become Jesus's disciples. Clay, who had recently come to faith in Jesus, was with us, along with his wife. At one point, he told me I was going to see a transformation. He brought out a brimmed hat and put it on. He said it was his "concert hat," and when he put it on, he became "Concert Clay." I didn't know what he meant until the drinks started going down one after another. By the time the concert began, he was pretty lit up.

"Anybody got some doobie?" Clay asked (that's a marijuana joint, in case you didn't know). "Anybody got some doobie? We want some doobie over here! We're gonna party tonight. Come on, let's go!" He was running all over the place, putting his arm around anyone who was next to him.

I ran with him to try to keep him out of trouble. "No, that's all right, we don't want your doobie," I kept saying. "He's married, by the way. That's his wife up there." I stayed close to Clay wherever he went. I don't remember whether the Kings of Leon were any good that night because I was too busy watching out for Clay.

A few days later, after we had returned home from the concert, Randy came to me and said: "We've got to confront him, dude! That was horrible!"

"I know, I know. It was bad," I replied. "However, keep in mind, he's a brand-new disciple of Jesus. He's a baby in the faith, and babies make a lot of messes."

"Yeah, I know. But how else is he going to know that what he did was wrong? We have to confront him on this one or he's going to keep doing it!" Randy said.

I found myself agreeing with Randy, and yet, it seemed the Holy Spirit wanted to teach us something in this. "Slow down—ask me for help," I remember the Lord saying.

"How about this," I said to Randy. "What if we pray and ask the Holy Spirit to convict him of his sin?" I remembered Jesus saying that he would send his Spirit to do that (John 16:8–9). "Before we talk to Clay, let's talk to God and ask the Spirit to do his job. Let's wait a bit and see what he might do."

"I don't know if that is going to work!" Randy said.

I laughed to myself. I was thinking: "I believe he can do it. Jesus said he would. I sure hope he does."

So we prayed—and waited.

The following week at our missional community family meal, Clay didn't bring anything to drink, as he usually did. This happened again the next week, so I said to him: "Hey, I noticed you didn't bring or drink any alcohol the past couple of weeks. What's up?"

"I really hurt my wife and I embarrassed you guys at the concert," he said. "I don't think God wants me to party like that anymore. Concert Clay is dead. That's the old me. I'm not that guy anymore."

I looked across the room at Randy. With a stunned look on his face, he mouthed the words, "*No way!*" I think both of us were amazed. We were thinking, "The Spirit just did that!"

How many times have we tried to play the role of the Holy

Spirit in another person's life? Sure, there are times when we need to speak directly to one another about sin, but why not try speaking to God first, asking his Spirit to do the work? How will people ever learn to be led and filled with the Holy Spirit to overcome sin and temptation if we never allow space for him to do it?

This is an absolutely necessary step in our effectiveness on Jesus's mission. He promised he would send his Spirit to convict the world of sin, righteousness, and judgment (John 16:8). His mission cannot be accomplished without his Spirit doing that both in us and in others to whom we are sent.

Anointed to Preach

After Jesus overcame the temptation, he returned to Galilee in the power of the Holy Spirit and taught in the synagogues (Luke 4:14–15). On one occasion, he came to Nazareth and entered the synagogue. The scroll of the prophet Isaiah was given to him, and he opened it and read:

> "The Spirit of the Lord is upon me, because he has anointed me to proclaim good news to the poor. He has sent me to proclaim liberty to the captives and recovering of sight to the blind, to set at liberty those who are oppressed, to proclaim the year of the Lord's favor."
>
> And he rolled up the scroll and gave it back to the attendant and sat down. The eyes of all in the synagogue were fixed on him. And he began to say to them, "Today this Scripture has been fulfilled in your hearing." And all spoke well of him and marveled at the gracious words that were coming from his mouth. And they said, "Is not this Joseph's son?" (Luke 4:18–22)

These people had watched Jesus grow from a baby to a man. He had done nothing like this before. Suddenly he was speaking with incredible authority and making some audacious claims. "Who is this kid?" they asked one another. "Isn't he Joseph's son? We've watched him grow up. He's never done anything like this! What's going on?"

What *was* going on?

Jesus told them, "The Spirit of the Lord has anointed me to preach."

How did Jesus preach with such authority and power? It was by the Spirit, who had anointed him.

The same thing happened to Jesus's disciples at Pentecost after he had ascended to heaven. Luke gives us a very detailed account of Jesus's ministry as Jesus was filled with and led by the Holy Spirit. Then he gives a detailed account of the early church's ministry as they were filled with and led by the Holy Spirit. Both ministries look the same because it was the same Spirit.

Jesus told the disciples to wait in Jerusalem for the Holy Spirit, "for John baptized with water, but you will be baptized with the Holy Spirit not many days from now" (Acts 1:4–5). Then he said to them, "You will receive power when the Holy Spirit has come upon you, and you will be my witnesses in Jerusalem and in all Judea and Samaria, and to the ends of the earth" (v. 8).

"As the Father has sent me, even so I am sending you."

When the Spirit filled the first disciples, all 120 of them, men and women, young and old, proclaimed the mighty deeds of God in languages all of the visitors to Jerusalem could understand. Then Peter got up to explain it, and in the power of the Holy Spirit, he preached a message through which more than three thousand people came to faith in Jesus and were added to the family of God in one day (Acts 2). It wasn't an incredibly well-written and well-prepared message. It was a Spirit-empowered message that led to thousands becoming disciples of Jesus.

Jesus preached by the power of the Holy Spirit. The church did so as well.

So can we.

You and I, if we have the Spirit of Christ, have the same power to proclaim the good news of Jesus as Jesus did. You don't need a seminary degree or a Bible school education. You don't need a title or position. Jesus's disciples had none of these. But they had been with Jesus, and Jesus was with them by his Spirit.

He is with you, too.

I love it when Christians who are filled with the Spirit proclaim the good news of Jesus as his sent ones. It's so fun to hear them try to explain what they said. They generally say: "Well, it was like this . . . I said . . . Well, I can't quite repeat it as I said it . . . It was like . . . Oh, you had to be there." That's because the Spirit gave them the words and the power they needed in that moment to share Christ with someone else. That's what he does. What a privilege to have God use our mouths to proclaim Jesus with power and authority to others!

He wants to do that through you by his Spirit because you are his missionary.

Displaying the Good News

Jesus went on to heal the sick, raise the dead, and cast out demons, all by the power of the Holy Spirit. Jesus displayed the good news of the kingdom.

We have the same Spirit. We have the same power. We can do the same things as the Holy Spirit fills, leads, and empowers us. Jesus said so himself before he taught his disciples about the Spirit: "Truly, truly, I say to you, whoever believes in me will also do the works that I do" (John 14:12). There are far too many people in the church who do not believe this truth, and as a result, they either lack the power for the mission or just disengage from Jesus's mission to the world altogether.

Let's think through our four questions again. *Who is God?* He is Spirit. *What has he done?* He sent and empowered Jesus the Son to take on flesh and to seek and save what was lost. *Who are we?* We are missionaries, sent and empowered by the same Spirit. If we believe this, *what do we do?* We make disciples of Jesus through proclaiming the gospel in the power of the Spirit.

If you are a child of God and a servant of King Jesus, you have been sent into the world as his missionary with the same Spirit that sent and empowered Jesus.

Several months after the Kings of Leon concert, Clay found out that he had a large mass wrapped around the lower part of his spinal cord. He was told that surgery was necessary and it was very possible that he would never walk again. So Clay decided to head to Southern California for some surfing, perhaps the last time he would ever surf. He told me he ran into a church that was baptizing people on the beach. One of the guys doing the baptizing introduced himself as Rick. I asked Clay if his last name was Warren. He said, "Yes, that was his name—Rick Warren." I laughed and said, "God's surrounding you, brother!" Rick Warren is pastor of Saddleback Church, one of the largest churches in the United States.

The night before Clay went into surgery, he asked us to pray for his healing. "God still does that, right?" he asked. "That's the stuff Jesus does, and if he's in us, he can still do that, right?"

I said, "Yes, Clay, Jesus still can heal." So we prayed. I'll never forget watching my children lay hands on Clay along with us as we prayed for his healing.

The next day, we arrived at the hospital to find out that

when the doctors had opened Clay's back, the mass was completely gone!

Jesus still heals! He healed Clay!

Jesus said that part of the church's mission was to show that submission to his rule and reign changes things. God gives his Spirit to us to enable us to experience the power of Jesus in very real ways so that we don't just preach a message about God's power to save, but we help people experience his power.

When we finally got in to visit Clay, he was asleep because of the pain medication, so a few of us from our missional community waited in his room for him to wake up. The guy in the next bed asked: "Who is this guy? Is he a pastor or something?"

"Why?" we asked.

"Well, he's been talking to me about Jesus."

"What did he say?" we asked. The man went on to describe how Clay had told him the story of Jesus saving him and then healing him. Clay had been sharing the good news about Jesus! He was a disciple who was beginning to live out his new identity as a missionary.

When Clay woke up, he could hardly believe that he had shared the gospel like that. We reminded him: "You have the Spirit now, and that's what he does through us. He loves to brag on Jesus; in fact, there is no one better at bragging on Jesus than his Spirit. He's known him forever and loves him more than anyone."

You may not experience the kind of miraculous healing that Clay did or even get to see someone healed (though I encourage you to continue believing that God is as fully capable of healing through us as he was through Jesus's ministry), but if Jesus has changed you, you have something to live for and something to talk about. And you have the same Spirit who witnessed through the early disciples' mouths.

You are Jesus's missionaries, sent with his Spirit to proclaim the good news of Jesus with authority and boldness. That is why Jesus gave you his Spirit—so you could be his witnesses (Acts 1:8).

Clay had his ups and downs over the years. Once I became very frustrated that he did not seem to be growing much in his faith. He and his family were hardly ever at our weekly meal. They missed most Sunday gatherings. He was no longer a part of our DNA group. I was very concerned that he was just walking away from Jesus.

I shared my concerns with Jayne, and she replied, "Well, are you praying for him?"

I love my wife! She's a huge gift to me. I needed to hear the same words I had spoken to Randy earlier.

So I returned to praying for Clay. The Spirit is so much better at this than we are. He is the better missionary and the better discipler.

Shortly thereafter, I was coming back from an early morning meeting when an ambulance and a couple of fire trucks passed me. I had an immediate impression, "Go to Clay's house!" I believe it was the Spirit leading me. So I drove there, praying all the way. Sure enough, the ambulance and trucks were parked in front of his house. I immediately scanned the area for Clay or his family. His wife was standing outside, and it looked as if she was crying. "Oh, no!" I thought. "I hope nothing horrible has happened to Clay." Clay's wife fell onto my shoulder in tears. So I asked: "Is Clay all right? What's happened?"

She went on to tell me that the man across the street had hung himself in his garage. Clay was just walking outside to take his daughter to school when the man's girlfriend had come out screaming. Clay ran into the garage and tried to get the man down. Clay told me later that though the man's hair was normally gray, it had turned jet black. His cheeks were fire red, and it felt as if he weighed 800 pounds, though he was only a 180-pound man. Clay believes some kind of demonic work was going on in that garage and in this man's life. Clay didn't know what to do, so he prayed. Then he saw a pair of scissors in the corner. He cut the rope with which the man had hung himself, then lowered him down. There was no pulse and no breathing. Clay administered CPR for a while, but nothing happened.

The man was gone. Dead.

So Clay stepped back and prayed one more time: "If it's his time to go, Father, take him home. If not, in the name of Jesus, bring him back to life!" At that moment, Clay felt a power come into the room and the man started breathing again.

He was alive!

This reignited Clay's walk with God. How could it not?

I remember him saying to another man from Soma, "I wonder if God is trying to show me that I am supposed to start reaching out to my neighbors."

Yes, Clay, that is why you were given God's Spirit and power—to do the work God both saved you and sent you to do.

The same Spirit that raised Jesus from the dead was at work in Clay. He is also in us to work through us if we belong to Jesus.

Shortly after this, a woman who is now a part of our missional community was working at the hospital, serving at the bedside of this same man. She had heard how God had rescued him through Clay, and she told him that God had physically saved him so that he could hear about God's salvation through Jesus Christ. She went on to share the gospel with him right there in the hospital room.

Healing; light coming into the darkness; the dead coming to life; gospel proclamation in a hospital—all done by the power of the Holy Spirit.

"As the Father has sent me, even so I am sending you."

Always on Mission

We have the Spirit of God in us so that we might be empowered, just as Jesus was. We are his missionaries, filled and anointed by his Spirit. If you have the Spirit of God, you are a missionary sent by Jesus to tell the world who he is and what he has done.

Charles Spurgeon said, "Every Christian is either a missionary or an imposter."[1] Everywhere you go, whatever you do, you are a missionary sent by Jesus to love like Jesus, overcome sin like Jesus, proclaim the gospel like Jesus, and see people's lives changed by the power of the Spirit that raised Jesus from the dead.

You are always on mission. Every part of your life, every activity and event, is part of Jesus's mission to make disciples.

Remember, you are not alone on this mission. Jesus goes with you everywhere because his Spirit is in you to empower you to be his representative in the world. He wants to saturate your world in Word and deed by his presence at work in and through you by his Spirit.

Our baptism is a reminder of our new identity in Christ. We have been saturated with the Father, Son, and Holy Spirit. We have a new name because we are new creations that can do new works by the power of the Holy Spirit living in us. This is why Jesus places baptism first in the sequence of events of making disciples. He wants us to know who we are and what power we now have to do what he wants. His command for us to "[teach] them to observe all that I have commanded you" comes after we establish people in their new identity (Matt. 28:19–20).

Since you do who you are, you need to know who you are in Christ.

Knowing and believing who you are in Christ leads you to obey Jesus's commands.

---

[1] Charles H. Spurgeon, *The Sword and the Trowel: 1873* (London: Passmore & Alabaster, 1873), 56.

The people in our young, growing church didn't need a new to-do list. They needed to be reminded of their new identity in Christ. The same is true for you.

We are the Father's family; therefore, we love others like he loved us.

We are servants of Christ; therefore, we serve the least of these as he served us.

We are missionaries filled and empowered by the same Spirit that was in Jesus; therefore, we are always on mission to proclaim the good news of Jesus.

Whatever he has done to us, he now wants to do through us to others.

Part 5

The Everyday Stuff

Everyday Rhythms

"This is Jeff. You know, that pastor I told you about who isn't really like a pastor." That's how Amy, our neighbor, introduced me to Clay and Kristie. We were at Amy and Tully's house for a Halloween party, and Clay and Kristie had just arrived. It seemed Amy and Tully had been talking to them about Jayne and me. Amy and Tully didn't agree with our views about Jesus and they weren't very fond of church leadership or the church in general, but they had become good friends of ours. We had spent a lot of time together in the everyday stuff of life—sharing meals, watching one another's children, caring for Nicki, celebrating holidays and special events together, and just doing life together. They wanted some more of their friends to meet us.

Let's go back to that conversation Caesar and I had in the warehouse, the conversation where I said we had an identity problem.

During that time, we realized that many were still struggling with the default mode of seeing church primarily as an event. It seemed people knew how to engage in the activities of the church when we gathered and even how to do the mission when we organized for it. But they didn't know how to live in the everyday stuff of life with gospel intentionality. They couldn't see the things they were already doing as great opportunities to show what everyday life in submission to Jesus could look like.

Seeing church mainly as an event creates a significant problem for mission, because most people are very busy. And the more we fill our lives with church events and programs, the more we get pulled out of everyday life with people who don't yet know Jesus. Besides, we will never be able to live out our identities of family, servants, and missionaries in one or two church events a week. It must involve everyday life. We need to see that life is the program, because people need to see what it means to follow Jesus in the everyday stuff of life.

We realized we needed to help our people see that life has a normal rhythm. All people everywhere are engaged in things that happen in rhythm—day in and day out. When we engage in these everyday rhythms with Jesus-centered, Spirit-led direction, mission can happen anytime and everywhere, and anybody can be a part of it.

We needed to train people how to live everyday life with gospel intentionality, showing what it looks like to follow Jesus in the normal stuff.

So we asked ourselves: "What are the everyday rhythms of life that everybody engages in everywhere? How can we engage in what is already going on? And how does our submission to Jesus change how we do it?" We knew that if we identified the everyday rhythms of life and trained people to engage in them in light of the gospel with the purpose of making disciples, they would be better equipped to be disciples of Jesus anywhere and everywhere.

Six Regular Rhythms

What are the everyday rhythms? What do humans do daily, weekly, or monthly?

We eat, work, play, rest, celebrate, create, interact, give, and do many other things. As we brainstormed, we wrote these and many more activities on a whiteboard. We knew we shouldn't try to identify too many or people would be overwhelmed. We decided to simplify our list to six.

We ended up with these: Eat, Listen, Story, Bless, Celebrate, and ReCreate.

Eat

Everybody eats at least three times a day in most places. Eating is not an extra event added on to your life. What if you ate with others more often? What if you regularly shared meals with people who loved Jesus, as well as with those who don't yet know and love him?

Something very significant happens at a meal. We are hungry. We are in need. And that need is met only by something outside of our bodies. It's interesting that Jesus called himself "the bread of life" (John 6:35). We have a deep spiritual hunger that can be met only by Jesus. Every meal can be a reminder of this. What if God's intent in having us remember Jesus through a meal was to help us remember him through every meal? (1 Cor. 11:17–34).

When people eat together, they experience something more than a physical event. A spiritual event takes place, whether they acknowledge it or not. God has provided a means to sustain life outside of our own lives, and whenever we eat, we are experiencing God's care and provision.

Jews were known for blessing God for the ground that received the seed, the farmer who sowed the seed, the rains that fell on the soil, the sun that warmed the soil, the worker who harvested the wheat, the baker who turned it into bread, and the means they were given to purchase this bread. The meal was a time to pause, raise one's hands high, and worship the Giver of the bread through thanksgiving.

It's interesting that many in our culture bless the meal, but not the Giver of the meal. Maybe it's because at one time, there was real reason for concern about getting sick from a meal. Today, you should no longer be concerned—unless, of course, you're eating fast food.

A meal should be a worship event! Don't bless the food, bless the Giver of the food!

Whether we acknowledge it or not, something unseen also happens between people when they eat together. Their common need is met with a common provision. The meal creates an experience of unity—of oneness at a table. This is why most business deals take place during meals and why more conversation happens when people have drinks in their hands or are sitting together around a table. This is also why Jesus was called a friend of sinners—he identified with them over meals (Matt. 11:19). And this is why the Lord's Supper or Eucharist is also called Communion—it is a common meal eaten together to remind us of a common provision we share. We are one in our need and one in taking in God's provision for our need—thus, we have communion.

This was how we got to know Amy and Tully. After we had lived in our home for several months, the rain in the Northwest subsided and people started coming out of their caves to see the bright round light in the sky again and make up for their vitamin D deficiency. With the warming weather, we decided to host a cookout every Friday night for the summer. At first, hardly anyone came. We were told people didn't get together to eat in our neighborhood. But we didn't let that stop us. Every

Thursday, Haylee, who was three at the time, and I knocked on doors and invited people to join us. It's hard for people to say no to a little girl as cute as Haylee!

I remember one neighbor finally said, after a few of our attempts, "You're not gonna give up, are you?"

I said: "Of course not! Not until you've come on over!"

Those meals brought our neighbors together. They brought Amy and Tully, along with their daughters, and us together. And they led to their hosting parties themselves.

Eventually, those meals led to our meeting Clay and Kristie on Halloween.

Eat meals together—regularly.

You're already eating, probably three times a day. Don't do it alone. Do it with others and watch Jesus join you at the table and change the meal. He's well acquainted with joining people at the table. Invite him to dinner with a few others and see what he does.

This is an easy step for you or your group to take. Start eating together. And eat with those who don't yet know Jesus. You will find that many opportunities will open up at the table.

Listen

Everybody is listening all the time. But who or what are we listening to, and are we paying attention to what we're hearing?

As God's people, we have his Spirit in us, regularly speaking to us through the Scriptures as we read them and recall them; through his church as we interact with one another; and personally as we listen closely to his voice (in John 10:1–21, Jesus said his sheep hear and listen to his voice, and in John 14–15, he said his Spirit would be the means by which we abide with him and are led by him).[1]

[1] Since the Spirit of God is the same One who inspired the writing of Scripture, we should always test what we hear to make sure it does not contradict God's written Word. God will not speak to

So the first question is this: Are you listening to God's Spirit through his Word, his community, and his personal communication to you directly?

Second, who or what is the loudest voice in your life? Is it God's Spirit, or is it someone or something else? You won't be able to join God in his work all around you if you aren't paying attention to him.

So we need to listen for our own good, but others need us to listen to them. One of the greatest gifts we can give one another is a set of open ears and a closed mouth. Sure, there are times to speak, but are we willing to listen to one another?

People in the United States spend billions of dollars on counseling or mental-health care each year. Certainly some of this care needs to be given by professionally trained counselors. However, large numbers of the people seeking counseling are primarily looking for others to listen to them.

I have found that listening is one of my greatest acts of faith and dependency on God. It reminds me that he is at work even when I'm not talking—maybe more so. Proverbs 10:19 says, "When words are many, transgression is not lacking, but whoever restrains his lips is prudent."

Listening also reminds me that the Spirit can speak to others in our silence. In fact, our willingness to quiet our souls and care for others often creates the best space for the Spirit to work. One of Jesus's titles is "Wonderful Counselor" (Isa. 9:6). He said that when he left he would send "another Counselor" (John 14:16 RSV), the Holy Spirit, to come and dwell in us. If you are a child of God, you have the Counselor living in you. Listen to him! And listen to others.

It was time for all the kiddos to go trick-or-treating. It was also starting to drizzle outside. Halloween in the Northwest is dark and often wet.

us in ways contrary to His written Word. We also should regularly submit ourselves and what we believe God is saying to us to a community of people who know and submit to God's Word.

The dads were sent out into the rain to oversee the candy fetching. I walked with Clay, and as we walked, I asked about his life, where he grew up, what his upbringing was like, what he was doing at present, what he loved. Then I listened. I learned about Clay and I found him to be very interesting.

People *are* interesting. If we will listen, we will discover this.

They are image bearers of God. They are broken, marred, and not fully together, just like us—but they are image bearers nonetheless. It's amazing, when you take the time to listen, how much you can learn. You begin to see how amazingly unique and creative each one of God's image bearers is.

I can't tell you how many times I heard Clay refer to energy—"I really like the energy I feel there" or "That person has some great energy"—and light—"Did you ever notice how some people seem to have more light than others?" I also came to understand what Clay valued, including faithfulness in relationships; tangible, hands-on expressions of kindness through serving; and his children's futures.

By listening, I showed Clay I cared. I learned how he communicated and what certain concepts meant to him. I also got to know his story. He let me in as I listened, and as a result, I discovered how the good news of Jesus could be good news for Clay in light of his past brokenness and present longings.

I couldn't see it, but the Spirit was also working while I was listening.

Quiet your soul and listen to God. And close your mouth once in a while and listen to others. Do both together, and you will find yourself joining in with the activity of the Spirit working through you as his dwelling place. Remember, you are the temple of the living God! If you will listen, people will find themselves meeting with God when they are with you, even though they are not fully aware of it. We have God to give to people. Why would we want to get in the way of that by talking the whole time we are with them?

Are you familiar with God's presence in your life? Do you recognize his voice?

Do you set aside regular time to listen to God through his Word, by his Spirit? Open the Bible and take time to invite him to speak to you through it, then write down what he says to you.

Do you listen to God on others' behalf? What is he saying about them to you?

Do you listen to others when you are with them? What are they saying and what is the Spirit saying?

Listen. He is speaking, and so are they. Open your ears as an act of love.

Story

Everybody lives in light of a larger story. They are rehearsing these stories in their minds all of the time, and the stories provide the lenses through which people view their worlds. A person's dominant story will significantly shape his beliefs, behaviors, and everything in his life.

The dominant stories for most people are their family stories—the unique contexts in which they grew up. Randy's view of God as Father was primarily shaped by his life with his earthly father. As a result, Randy had a very hard time going to God in prayer and calling on him as Father. Until Randy repented of (turned from) his father as the primary story of what a father is like and turned to Jesus as the picture of what the true Father is like, his primary story was not based upon the gospel—the true and better story. I knew his story and I knew the gospel story. As I listened to Randy, I also listened to the Spirit as he brought to remembrance the biblical story of God as a perfect Father expressed through Jesus the Son. This enabled me to lead Randy to Jesus to correct this part of his story. The larger narrative of God's story can bring redemption to each of our individual stories.

We should all know God's story and regularly rehearse it to ourselves and to one other. We need to be regularly in God's Word, the Bible, in order to be acquainted with his story.

We also need to listen well to others' stories so we are able to bring the good news of God's redemptive story to bear on the stories of those who don't yet know how God can redeem their brokenness.

After that Halloween night in the rain, we had another meal or two with Clay and Kristie. At these meals, we, along with others from our missional community, listened and learned more about their story. In a very short time, they grew to trust us. Meals with open ears and genuine love will do that.

I'll never forget the day when Clay asked if Jayne and I, along with our children, wanted to join their family for a weekend on the ocean in a beach house together. This doesn't happen in the Northwest generally. People aren't usually that open with their lives and vacation time. So we said yes. Something more than a mere acquaintance was going on here.

The first afternoon, we all hung out on the beach. The kids played in the sand and the adults watched Clay try to surf. He never got up and almost drowned from exhaustion. It was both funny and a little frightening to watch, wondering if he would make it.

While we were walking along the beach, laughing about Clay's near escape from a watery grave, he said: "I love the power of the waves. There's something there. Some kind of energy I feel. What do you think that is?"

I said: "Well, Clay, I believe God created all of this and designed it so that it would all point to him, displaying what he is like. He also made you and designed you to experience it and then give him credit for all of it. You are feeling the power of the wave, and God designed it to tell you that he is powerful. The energy you feel is coming from him. And the reason you like it so much is because he made you for himself—to worship him. The wave, along with all of creation, is God's way of saying: 'Hey! I'm here! I made all of this, and it is telling you what I am like. Turn to me and thank me for what I've done. I want you to know me and worship me.' Clay, God is trying to get your attention through that wave, and he wants you to give him credit for making it and causing it to display part of what he is like."

I'll never forget Clay's response: "Well, I don't know if I believe that . . . but I believe there is something behind that energy I feel when I'm out there." Clay was very typical of those who live in the Northwest. He grew up not believing in the God over nature, but with a view of nature as godlike.

He needed a new story—the true and better story.

We headed back to the house, ate dinner together, put the kids to bed, and then joined each other in the hot tub. At that point, Clay spoke up: "We want to let you know why we invited you out here."

"Here we go," I thought. "Please don't let this be something weird! This could go south really fast!"

By the way, this "everyday life on mission" stuff can be unpredictable or messy. I often share that if it isn't messy here and there, you are likely not yet on mission. If you are becoming friends with people who don't yet know and love Jesus, you are going to be invited into experiences that may be very different from what you're used to.

Clay continued: "Emma has been asking us about God and we don't really know what to tell her. I know you believe in God and all that, so what do you think we should tell her?"

Phew! I was relieved and overjoyed! This was what we had hoped and prayed for.

"First of all," I said, "I want you to know, Clay, that God wants you to be a spiritual leader in your home. It is your job to teach your children about who God is and what he has done. So I'm glad you are asking about how to do that. Pay attention, so you can lead your children well."

Discipleship was beginning—on the beach, in a hot tub, in the everyday stuff of life. We were leading Clay and Kristie, even before they believed, into what life as a disciple of Jesus would be like.

I went on to share the story of God from Genesis to Revelation: God created. Humans rebelled. God pursued humanity and called a people to himself. Eventually, through that people, a child was born, the God-man, Jesus. He came to live the perfect life we cannot, to die in our place so we can be forgiven, and to rise again from the grave to deliver us from sin and death. One day he will return to bring about a final judgment and a new creation, where all who belong to him will enjoy new life with him forever. It took about ten minutes to go through the whole story.

Then I told Clay that we are living in the time between what God has already done through Jesus's life, death, and resurrection and what he will do in the end. He is still writing his story, and what we were doing in that moment, in that hot tub, was also part of it. I shared with him that God was pursuing Clay and his family through us. This was part of his story as well.

Jayne also shared that we had purchased *The Jesus Storybook Bible* by Sally Lloyd-Jones to give to them. We encouraged them to read it with their children every day if possible so that they could learn more about God's pursuit of them through Jesus.

Do you know the story of God? Could you tell it to someone if they asked?[2]

---

[2] To learn more about the story of God, please visit www.saturatetheworld.com/story-of-god

Do you know the story of those with whom you are on mission? How about your friends who don't yet personally know the love of God?

Do you know how to tell your story and show how Jesus is the hero who redeemed your story?[3]

Let's recap:

Eat meals together with disciples of Jesus and with those who need to be.

Listen to the Word, to others, and to the Spirit of God, and pay close attention.

Know and rehearse God's story, learn others' stories, and consider how aspects of God's story can bring redemption and restoration to theirs.

And tell your story, making sure Jesus is the hero.

Bless

Everybody has been blessed. And God's people know they have been blessed to be a blessing. We give from what we have to others in the form of words, actions, or tangible gifts. Such blessing is not meant to be a once-in-a-while deal. God intends for us to live in a perpetual rhythm of blessing others.

This truth is one of the distinctives of God's people throughout God's story. Whatever God gives to his people, he plans to give through them to others who need what they have. We have been blessed to be a blessing.

As we eat with one another, we listen and learn about one another's stories. Sometimes we need to speak a better story into their lives. Sometimes we need to bring a blessing as a demonstration of how God's story has changed our lives. When we really come to know one another's stories, we also come to

---

[3] For help telling your own story, making Jesus the hero, please visit www.saturatetheworld.com/hero-of-my-story

know how we can best bless one another, because we know what others really need.

The members of one of our groups responded to this teaching by making a list of all that they had been given. They put large Post-it notes on the walls and wrote on them everything they had: financial savings, investments, homes, extra rooms, vehicles, tools, skills, experiences, training, time—the lists were packed with a plethora of blessings.

Then they asked, "What are the needs in this group?" They assumed that God had given them everything they needed. They just needed to give it away to one another. I'll never forget one of the responses. A few of the people were honest and shared that they really didn't have financial resources to help others because they had some significant credit card debt. It didn't take long for the group to speak up: "We have the resources to pay these debts off. Let's do this!" Those with money had been blessed in order to bless those who were in debt. They paid off all of their credit card debts. Those who were blessed with good money-management skills then blessed them by teaching them how to build budgets, stay out of debt, and better steward their resources.

I love this because blessing shows the heart of God—it is a tangible picture of what he has done for us. Jesus removed the great debt of our sin through his death on the cross so we might be debt free—fully forgiven. Now we get to bless others in light of his rich blessing. Peter instructed Christians who were living a radically different life of submission to authority and blessing to others to "honor Christ the Lord as holy" (1 Pet. 3:15). He was referring to setting Christ apart in their hearts as the one they would live for, as well as the primary example for how they should live. He went on to say that they should always be "prepared to make a defense to anyone who asks you for a reason for the hope that is in you."

Another way of saying all of this is: *Live in such a way that it would demand a "Jesus explanation."* In other words, you wouldn't be able to explain what you do or why without needing to talk about Jesus. That's what this group had done. There was no way to explain their actions without also needing to talk about Jesus.

What if everyone in your group agreed to at least three tangible blessings a week? Three blessings from everyone in the form of word, deed, or gift would create plenty of opportunities to share the good news of Jesus.

We invited Clay and Kristie into this life of blessing. They joined in with us as our missional community paid to have Nicki's van repaired, covered her utility bill when she couldn't afford it, or visited her in the hospital when she became sick. Clay's dad also became ill and needed to move in with Clay and Kristie. We found out that Clay was remodeling the second floor of his home so he and Kristie could move upstairs and give their bedroom to Clay's dad. The group stepped up and helped to move furniture, tear out walls, and carry an old cast-iron tub down the steep staircase (I think I almost ruined my back on that one). Thankfully, some of the group members had some carpentry skills with which to serve.

We had been blessed to be a blessing.

Each time Clay and Kristie asked, "Why are you doing this?" we were able to tell them: "Jesus loved us. He paid to have our lives repaired with his own life. Jesus served us by laying his life down for us."

What's the reason for blessing? Jesus. We bless because he first blessed us. Now he blesses others through us.

Have you stopped to reflect on the number of ways you have been blessed? Take some time and write down the blessings you have received. Try this with a group, and then ask whether anyone in the group needs what you have. Next, ask whether there is anyone outside of your group who needs to receive from what you've been given.

Ask the Spirit to show you who to bless and how to bless them. Listen, and then bless with words, actions, or gifts.

Celebrate

Everybody engages in some form of celebration, from birthday parties to national holidays. Disciples celebrate the grace of God given to us through Jesus in order to express how good and gracious God is.

As people made in the image of God, we were created to celebrate. God celebrates. He parties! When God created, he celebrated. He said, "This is very good!" God's Word also directs us to celebrate his good work with him.

Today, God's people look back to what God has done for us through Jesus and forward to what we will enjoy forever in Jesus's presence. We celebrate these blessings. Jesus actually compared his kingdom to a great party (Matt. 22:1–2). One day, we will have an amazing celebration, with Jesus at the center of the party (Rev. 19:6–9).

Just as Jesus brought the better wine to the party at Cana (John 2:1–11), we also should bring what is lacking to the celebrations in our culture. One day, one of our pastors went to Wright Park in Tacoma to play basketball with his sons. When he arrived, he saw that a big party was going on. It was Tacoma's "Out in the Park" event—a gay-pride celebration. He confided to me that he was a little concerned that he might be wrongly perceived as a guy trying to pick up a date or that another Christian might see him there and wrongly judge him. He told me that he then heard the Spirit telling him: "I brought you here to love and serve these people. Stay. Ask them what they need." (He was listening.) So he found someone in charge and asked if they needed help. He was told that someone was needed to oversee the bounce house. So he and his kids served at the bounce house that day.

He brought the better wine. Jesus was there in him, loving people through his service. He was bringing what they lacked in a generous and loving way.

Sometimes it isn't necessary for us to bring something to the party. Sometimes we need to take up the servant towel for cleanup. Jesus did this prior to the Passover feast by stripping down to take on the posture of a servant sent to wash his disciples' feet (John 13:1–11). He said he was setting an example for us. He also stated: "A new commandment I give to you, that you love one another: just as I have loved you, you also are to love one another. By this all people will know that you are my disciples, if you have love for one another" (vv. 34–35).

One of our groups thought through how they could bring the servant towel to the pub crawl in their community. You know what a pub crawl is, right? People go from pub to pub, drinking and drinking, until they are crawling. The group realized the servant towel involved providing rides home for people too drunk to drive. They gave the bartenders their contact info, plastered the bathroom walls with fliers, and set up shop near the bars with coffee and vans ready to drive people home (I told them, only half joking, that they should probably cover their seats with plastic). The bartenders were blown away! Who does this? The church does!

No one died that night.

Sometimes there is no party where there should be one. That discovery prompted the missional community to throw birthday parties for all the children whose single moms couldn't afford to. That was why we invited Nicki to participate in Thanksgiving or Christmas with us when we realized she had no one with whom she could celebrate.

The better wine. The servant towel. The party in the absence of one.

The kingdom is like a party. And we are the party people, because we belong to the King who parties. He is the best at celebrating.

When my fortieth birthday came around, Jayne decided to throw me a party. It was truly amazing, a picture of the kingdom. Jayne is an artist, so she painted a picture of me (it was a little awkward looking at a likeness of myself when I entered the party). The place was fully decorated. A bunch of the guys wore mullet wigs (I had a mullet in high school, and Jayne thought it would be funny to make sure everyone knew that). The food and drink were amazing! So was the music. Jayne hired a very talented DJ who once worked at raves and now lived among our community. They roasted me through songs, pictures, crazy stories, and skits, in which they imitated me at different stages of my life.

Then, at the end, after they had fully roasted me, they took time to toast me. All those who were part of our community and loved Jesus highlighted his work in and through my life.

A man raised a glass: "Jeff, I want to toast your kindness to others. Clearly Jesus has been kind to you and is working through you to be kind." He then gave several examples.

Another said: "Jeff, I raise a glass to the way you serve people. You are a great picture of how Jesus has served us!"

Amy stood up and raised her glass: "You know I don't believe any of this. However, if I were ever to become a Christian, I would want to be like you, Jeff."

Wow! I was so encouraged.

Then Clay stood up. "I don't know about all of this," he said. "I do know I see light in you. I feel a good energy in you. I even feel drawn by that energy and light. I'm not really sure yet what that is, but whatever it is, I toast to that!" I thought, "You're not far from the kingdom, Clay!"

Finally, I stood up and said, "It's my party; I can preach if I want to." My friends, both Christian and non-Christian, laughed. I went on: "I want to raise my glass to Jesus. This party is great because of him. There is no way people from all these backgrounds with differing beliefs would ever come together and have this much fun if it weren't for Jesus. He brings people together. Nor would the things you said about me be true if it weren't for how he has changed my life. He is the King of the party and he made this a great party! Clay, the light and energy in me that you toasted, that light is Jesus and that energy is his Spirit! So I'm joining you in toasting Jesus. The greatest gift I could receive tonight is for you all to come to know the love Jesus has for you like I have. Raise your glass! To Jesus!"

Then we drank to Jesus our King!

I think a few of my non-Christian friends were a little nervous. They were probably wondering, "Did we just become Christians?" Not yet, but they were getting a taste of the kingdom and the greatness of our King. The Bible says we are to taste and see that the Lord is good (Ps. 34:8)! We gave them a taste that night.

How are you doing at celebrating? Do your parties show what the King and his kingdom are like? What celebrations are happening around you? Are people thankful that Jesus's disciples showed up at the party, because the party got better after you arrived? Maybe they need you to bring or be the better wine. Maybe some servants of Jesus need to bring the servant towel. Which parties need to happen where you live? What should be celebrated that isn't being celebrated?

How can you engage in the rhythm of celebration where Jesus has sent you?

ReCreate

ReCreate is our word for the rhythm of "rest and create." Everybody works and rests, creates and plays. Some, however, are not at rest when they create and work. Some rarely, if ever, just play.

Our God created and then rested. He didn't stop sustaining the universe and take a nap. His rest was a deep satisfaction with what he had created. His creation was very good. If you believe the good news of Jesus Christ, you also are able to truly rest. We can live with the confidence that God is running the world, so we don't have to. We can be settled at heart, knowing that Jesus has done all the work necessary to make us acceptable to God, so we no longer need to try to earn his acceptance through our work. We can work with all of our hearts unto the Lord out of gratitude, and actually be at rest while we are working.

If we believe the gospel, we can create amazing stuff as an outpouring of our new identity as new-creation people. In fact, those of us who are in Christ should be the most creative people, because we have been freed from enslavement to the approval of others, and we also are daily becoming more like our Creator. Because he has restored and is restoring us, we also are able to bring restoration to things broken, distorted, or marred by sin. This leads us to work in a state of rest, create at rest, and play at rest.

I have discovered that my lack of faith in God's power to save, sustain, and secure me is displayed in my lack of ability to truly rest, create, and play.

I will never forget a time when my children were very young. They wanted me to get down on the floor and play a game of Candy Land. I was busy running the world (that is, I was working) and I couldn't stop; how would the world keep running without me at the helm? Besides, who wants to play Candy

Land? There is no strategy unless you cheat and set up the cards when your kids are not looking. You just turn over a card and read the color.

"I guess I'm predestined to green on this one!"

"Wow! You got the Ice Cream Cone! You're almost to the end!"

"Bummer, I got the Gingerbread Man. I have to go backward!"

I agreed to play, but I could not rest or even enjoy my children. The entire time we were playing, I was thinking: "I have work to do! What's going to happen while I'm playing this game? I can't control anything in this game."

Then the Spirit tapped me: "I've got it. I'm running the world. Rest. Play. Enjoy your children. Trust me. I'm in control, and what I do is very good!"

I took a deep breath and asked the Spirit to help me walk in faith, to play at rest. And I rested.

The Israelites failed to enter into the rest God had for them due to their unbelief (Hebrews 3–4). I also failed to enter into rest because of my unbelief.

Are you able to play and create? Do you take a vacation, only to need a vacation from your vacation because your heart is screaming that you need to work, work, work to gain something?

When Clay and Kristie invited us to join them for that weekend away at the beach, I almost brought my computer just in case I had some time to do some work. The Spirit said, "No!" I left it home and I rested, believing God can do without me working. I also played with our children. God was gracious to grant me true rest, freeing me to play. We created sand castles for hours on the beach. It was a picture of true rest.

Too many of us can't rest and create. But we should be the most playfully rested people on the earth, because our Dad has it all taken care of for us!

Thankfully, Clay and Kristie saw rested, playful, creative people that weekend.

Later, we invited them into our restorative work, as we labored together to turn Nicki's backyard into a community garden.

As I said earlier, Nicki was a hoarder and her backyard was a jungle. We wanted to help her restore the inside of her house, but she wouldn't let us in while she was still alive. However, she did let us work on the backyard. Over several months, we transformed the yard into a community garden. Clay and Kristie were a part of that. It was an amazing transformation!

We rest, work, create, play, and restore, resting all the way.

Can you rest? I'm not talking about when you go to sleep at night or take a nap. Can you rest in the middle of your work, certain that you are accepted and loved, and have a Father in heaven that sees you and is proud of you?

Can you create freely, expressing the unique design your Creator intended you to be?

Can you play? Have you had much fun lately with your family or your community? Our Father wants us to be able to be carefree under his protection and provision, able to enjoy life.

Lastly, can you and your community creatively restore people or places in your community?

Everyday Life Is the Program

We continued to engage in these rhythms of life with gospel intentionality with Clay and Kristie, Nicki, and many others from our missional community and neighborhood.

Eat. Listen. Story. Bless. Celebrate. ReCreate.

One day, Clay called me and asked if he could join us at the warehouse where we met on Sundays. He'd never been to a gathering of the church, but he had come to my birthday party in that building. He asked if he needed to dress a certain way or become a member to attend. I told him to come however he wanted because all were welcome.

He didn't join us for a time, but for some reason, he decided to come on Easter Sunday. He didn't know it was a special day for us. Easter was all eggs, bunnies, and candy to him. There he was on Easter Sunday with his family, Kristie, Emma, and Keaghan. I preached my guts out, praying the whole time. To be honest, I was a little concerned that his attendance that day could change our relationship. Two years of life together, now this. What would happen?

After the gathering, I walked up to Clay. Kristie was a pool of tears next to him. He just stood there, looking as white as a ghost. I asked him how he was doing, and he just grunted and told me to give him space.

We didn't talk again until Tuesday. He called me and asked if I'd meet him in the community garden. I asked why, and he said he would tell me when we met.

When he arrived, right away he said, "I'm in!"

"What?" I replied.

"I'm in. I believe it!"

"Believe what?" I asked.

"I believe what you said on Sunday. I believe Jesus died on the cross for my sins. I believe I am forgiven."

I then asked him, "What are you experiencing personally right now from God?"

He said: "I know he loves me. I believe he's with me."

I told him: "That's his Spirit doing that. Remember the energy you saw in me? Now it's in you."

He said: "I know. I know what you mean now. So what do I do now?"

I said, "You need to tell our group and then get baptized." I went on to explain what baptism is.

He then said: "I want to do the stuff. You know, what you've all been doing. I want to give. How much do I give? I want to serve people like you did us. I want to tell others about Jesus, but I don't know how to do it like you did. I probably should get a Bible, don't you think?" He just went on and on.

He didn't need some class on how to be a disciple of Jesus. He had been in class for two years, watching us. Certainly he needed ongoing training, but he had been observing disciples following Jesus for a while already.

Life was the class. Everyday life was the program where he had been discipled to Jesus and discipled in what it looks like to follow Jesus.

If you have the Spirit of Christ Jesus, you are part of his body, the church. Everything you do matters. You are never alone. He is always with you. And because of this, you are always showing people what being a disciple—one who knows and loves Jesus—is like. You are making disciples every moment.

The real question is, "Who are you making disciples of?" Are you showing others what submission to Jesus in the normal stuff of life is like? Can they watch you, hang out with you, eat with you, and vacation with you, and see what it would be like if they were to love and obey Jesus in everyday life?

My parents had been doing that all those years, even though no one had told them that the best place to make disciples of Jesus is in the everyday rhythms of life. The students I had trained were doing it, too.

You can do it as well.

If you're part of a group, take some time to talk through how you can engage in these everyday rhythms on mission together to make disciples of Jesus in the everyday stuff of life.

Normal life is lived with gospel intentionality for the sake of seeing others come to know, love, and follow Jesus in normal life.

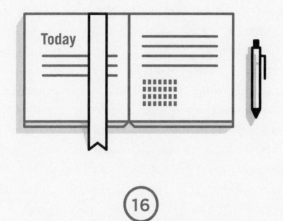

16

An Everyday Plan

"I can't accept that!" Alyssa exclaimed.

"Well, that's what a family does for one another," one of our group members reminded her.

Our missional community was in the midst of reforming our covenant for the next season together. Over the years, we have realized the need to refocus and reorient our groups on a regular basis, minimally once a year. We all experience mission drift. We can tend to forget who we are and what God has called us to do together. A missional community can subtly become primarily a support group that is only concerned about one another, forgetting the mission of making disciples of others. Some groups, especially if the members have been in the church for some time, gravitate toward only doing a Bible study together, so they need to be reoriented toward also obeying God's Word while on mission together.

We've also observed that missional communities can turn into social-activist groups, with little or no gospel proclamation—good deeds with no words about Jesus—while others may become outwardly focused on mission while failing to commit to seeing one another develop into maturity. Yet another ongoing challenge is keeping groups from expecting to accomplish everything we've talked about in a couple of hours a week and a special event here or there.

So we encourage our groups to reform their missional community covenants every year. Missional communities establish these covenants when they form in order to shape how they will live out their identities and rhythms in particular mission fields (see Appendix A: Missional Community Covenant Template, page 235). When our groups reform their covenants, they generally spend several weeks doing so, using our definition of a missional community—a family of missionary servants sent as disciples who make disciples—as a guide. The process moves through several steps:

Start with the Gospel

The first step is making sure we all still affirm our belief in the gospel of Jesus Christ. We don't want to ever assume this, so it is the first part of our covenant. In fact, we encourage our groups not only to affirm their individual and collective belief in the gospel, but also to develop a plan for rehearsing it together regularly. We want everyone to be fluent in the gospel, speaking it regularly to one another and to those who don't yet believe.

If you are part of a group, forming a group, or looking to reform a group, please make sure you build a strong gospel foundation and have a plan to help everyone become fluent in speaking the truths of Jesus into the everyday stuff of life.[1]

---

[1] For help with this, please visit www.saturatetheworld.com/gospel-fluency

Clarify the Mission

Next, we clarify our mission. We remind one another that we are commanded by Jesus to make disciples of all people groups. So we ask: "What people and place do we believe God is collectively sending us to this year? Who do we hope to see become followers of Jesus Christ?"

Our missional community has identified the faculty and families of Grant Elementary School, as well as the neighborhoods around it. Some groups focus on a neighborhood or region. Some focus on a particular group of people with common interests, experiences, or needs. The missional community in which Greg and Mary participate has identified families transitioning out of homelessness. Some of our artists are on mission to the artistic community, which is much more nomadic in nature. We have missional communities reaching out to college campuses, others that partner with Young Life to reach high school students, and some that see the local military base as their missional focus.

Recently, some of our leaders began a group that they call Dope Church. No, they are not smoking pot together during worship gatherings! One of the leaders has worked in the prison system for some time, and he recognized that upon their release, inmates often go back to using or dealing drugs or engaging in other illegal activity—even those who have come to faith in Jesus while behind bars. So some people got together and asked God how they could be on mission to and for these men and their families. This focus led them to a particular motel, where a lot of illegal drug dealing and sex trafficking took place. They determined that God was leading them to get on mission in that place, so they asked God to open a door for the gospel. Sure enough, the manager of this motel had been hoping someone would come to help, so he opened the door wide for the group members to love, serve, and share Jesus with the people engaging in illicit activities at the motel. They eventually called this outreach Dope Church.

Whom do you believe God is sending you to? Who around you needs to know Jesus? Is there a neighborhood or network of relationships where people need to be loved like family, served as Jesus served you, and told about the good news of salvation found in Jesus's name?

The possibilities for a missional focus are endless.

Some ask: "Why is having a missional focus so important? Isn't all of life mission? Isn't every one of us a missionary?"

Yes, all of life is mission and everyone is a missionary. Life is the mission trip. However, we've found it's important to also identify a collective mission—a missional focus. Too often, groups primarily talk about being on mission, but then the members leave the group meeting and find themselves alone on mission. As a result, many don't engage in mission, or if they do, they are lonely missionaries.

This was my dominant experience prior to starting Soma. Often I found myself in a weekly group meeting where each of us would share about friends who didn't yet know or believe in Jesus. Then we'd pray for one another and our individual missions to reach our friends. The rest of the week, we were alone, trying to share Jesus with our friends.

Very few people will lead others toward faith in Jesus all by themselves. It does happen, and each of us should always be ready to share the gospel. However, the biblical narrative provides very few examples of mission done in isolation. Jesus assembled his disciples on mission in groups of two or more. Paul traveled with a team. The early church was together daily on mission.

We need one another, and we need to be together in order for saturation to be accomplished most effectively.

A missional focus also provides common experiences through

which people can more effectively be trained. For instance, if we are all focusing on loving the faculty and families of Grant Elementary, our group will likely spend more time together at the school, engaging in common events and building overlapping relationships, and therefore experiencing more opportunities to be together for equipping in the everyday stuff of life.

Another strength of a common missional focus is that the people we are sent to can see what Jesus saves us into—the family of God. We are not just saved from hell. We are saved for God's purposes now into life together on his mission. So much of our missionary work fails because people hear a message but never see its implications (reconciliation into a loving family). We say the gospel has power to change our lives and relationships, but those with whom we share have no way of knowing this if they are never brought into a community that is experiencing it. Being on mission together consistently with a common focus provides a context in which to make disciples, as well as an experience of what life with Jesus is like.

Recently, our missional community, along with a few others, served at the Grant Elementary auction to raise money for art education. This elementary school, like many others, lost funding for the arts years ago. As a way to serve the teachers and students, parents host an auction to raise money to provide art supplies, training, and experiential learning. We've been actively involved with the auction for five years. This time, many of our members worked for several months in preparation and planning.

During the auction, twenty-two people from a few missional communities served. Many have no children at the school, and some are actually teachers at other schools. Several times throughout the night, those who were serving were asked: "Why are you doing this? You don't have any children at Grant Elementary. Why are you here? You're a teacher at another school? That makes no sense!" Each question provided an opportunity to talk about Jesus and his church.

One of the teachers at the school told Emily, one of the women who were serving: "I've been asking around about you. I'm trying to figure out why you would do this without any children at the school."

Emily explained: "Jesus has changed me, and because of his work in my life, I want to be used by him to show the world what he is like. Jesus's church is his people in the world who get to be a picture of what he is like, and our hope is that people will encounter the real Jesus, the Jesus of the Bible, not the one of religion."

This teacher answered: "I never encountered that Jesus in the church I went to growing up. There's got to be something we can do to repay you for all the work you've done to coordinate this evening."

Emily replied, "No, we're just here to serve, but if you really want to do something, I'll invite myself over to your house for dinner with your family to get to know you and your stories better."

The woman said, "You don't know what you just asked for, but if that's what you want, we will make it happen."

Many of us were asked similar questions throughout the night. Jesus was well represented through his body. This would not have been possible with an individualistic approach to mission.

A missional focus also helps us with our individual missions, as it gives each of us a context into which to invite our friends, a context where they can also experience the gospel being worked out in community on mission. For instance, one of the ways you could introduce your coworkers to Jesus is by inviting them to help with a service project your group is involved in within your missional focus—an auction, a community garden you're building, or a house you're restoring. This would provide an opportunity for your coworkers to experience what disciples of Jesus do, as well as how they interact as a loving family on mission together.

So how do you identify a missional focus?

I encourage the leaders of each new group to identify their focus, then call others to join them in the mission. If a group is already formed, I recommend praying, listening, and looking. Pray together for God to show you where he wants you to go, listen to what he says, and do it with your eyes wide open. This could include a night of prayer and brainstorming; prayer walks together, asking God to show you the harvest he is sending you to; or even an extended time of waiting on the Lord as a group to receive his direction. It's also helpful to consider where God has already granted you favor with some people who don't yet know and love Jesus or where he has opened a clear door of opportunity. If he has done this, you may want to start there. That's what happened with Dope Church: God opened a door, so the group started at the motel.

How do you know if you've identified a clear common missional focus? Ask yourselves: What are the rhythms of the people in this context? If you are able to identify their daily, weekly, monthly, and yearly rhythms of life *and* can articulate how your group could engage with the people within their established rhythms, you have likely identified a clear focus.

Keep in mind that you may be called to simply engage in the place where you are already involved and call others to join you. That is what Jayne and I have done. We are very invested in our children's school, so that is also our missional focus. Many of the others in our group would not naturally identify Grant Elementary as their missional focus, however. That's fine. They are with us for a season to be trained to make disciples, just like Jesus did with his disciples. When they are ready and have a heart for a particular people and place, we will send them out to start another missional community with some people who are called to their missional focus and others who need to be trained and sent elsewhere.

Form a Plan

Once we've clarified our mission, we walk through each of the identities, asking how we live in light of our identities in the everyday stuff of life. We generally spend at least one of our weekly meetings talking through each identity and how the gospel of Jesus informs who we are and how we should live out that identity in everyday rhythms (Eat, Listen, Story, Bless, Celebrate, and ReCreate). These discussions generally start with a short study from the Scriptures on the identity statement that week (for example, "We are God's family, who love like brothers and sisters," Ephesians 1; John 1:12–13; 13:34–35; Rom. 8:14–17; 1 John 4:7–8), followed by discussion about how we are going to live this identity out together. We usually have someone take notes so that we capture all that we come up with.

At the end of our three- to four-week process, we put the plan together and formally commit (some actually sign a document), with God's help, to faithfully fulfill it (note: we clarify that none of us will do this perfectly and that we all need the grace of the gospel to do it at all).

So, for instance, after studying about our identity as family, we might ask: "If we believe we are the family of God, how will we live like family in how often we *eat* together? How will we make time to *listen* to God through his Word and prayer? We all need to know his *story*; do we? If not, how will we all commit to grow in the study of God's Word? We also need to know one another's stories. How will we ensure that happens? In what ways do we believe we should *bless* one another with what we have? How will we *celebrate* God's grace together regularly? What kinds of celebrations will we have together, and how often? And how are we going to *recreate* through taking vacations, playing together, creating beauty, and restoring brokenness around us?"

In light of our missionary identity, we might ask: "How are we going to share meals with the people to whom God is sending us? Will we eat out at certain restaurants, have people over for dinner, do regular cookouts, or eat with them in other ways? And will we set aside regular time to pray for those we want to see come to know Jesus? When and how often? How do we expect to get to know their stories? When will we invite them to go through *The Story of God*[2] with us as a way of introducing them to God's redemptive plan through Jesus? In what other ways do we plan to share the gospel? Should we commit to ask God to give us at least one opportunity a day to share Jesus with someone else? And how has God blessed us to be a blessing to those to whom he is sending us? What do we have and what do they need? What celebrations are going on in this context and how can we bring the better wine to them? Finally, how can we engage in forms of recreation in our missional focus? What activities can we participate in? What needs beautification or restoration, and what will we do about it?"

Then, in light of our servant identity, we might ask: "How will we serve others through providing meals where necessary (the hungry, new mothers, the grieving)? How will we create space to listen to one another? From what we know of the story of this missional context, what are people's needs? How can we bless them in tangible ways and show them what the kingdom of God is like? Where do they need us to bring the servant towel to the celebration? Where are they lacking celebration, and how might we bring it? Lastly, who needs to experience

---

[2] To learn more about *The Story of God*, please visit www.saturatetheworld.com/story-of-god

rest? How might we serve them by providing opportunities for them to rest?"

If you engage in this activity with a group, you will find it very difficult and hugely beneficial.

It will be difficult because people will not immediately agree on everything. But they don't have to. In some cases, some in the group will want to commit to something, while others won't. That is fine, as people are in different places spiritually. The process will reveal levels of maturity and commitment, as well as fears, insecurities, selfishness, and pride.

It will be beneficial because, if this process is led well, much discipleship of one another will take place. Issues and concerns will come up, revealing where people need to be reminded of the gospel and its implications. Remember, conflict is not bad. It provides a context for discipleship to happen.

Keep in mind that you may not want everyone in the group going through this process together. You may have a core that is very committed to the mission and eager to engage this process, while others don't really want to. Don't necessarily try to get everyone to walk through these steps right away. Some just aren't ready.

Reforming Our Covenant

Our missional community had been on mission together in our neighborhood for several years, and Alyssa and Ian had recently joined our group. My first impression of Ian was that he was a Northwestern-style Rastafari hippie dude with dreads who wanted to save the environment. Alyssa struck me as a woman of the earth who loved everything organic and seemed to know how to make almost anything from stuff she found on their quarter-acre property. They didn't live in our neighborhood, but they had decided to join our group because they were friends with Paige and Adam, a couple in our missional community.

The previous summer, our missional community had decided to spend our weekly meal largely hanging out in our backyard, cooking on the grill and sitting around the fire pit. The summers are amazing in the Pacific Northwest. It stays light until around ten every night, so we found ourselves spending four to six hours together, eating, drinking, and talking around the fire. This provided an easy entry point for our friends to be introduced to the family. Alyssa and Ian had come several times to hang out around the fire with us, and gradually they found themselves wanting to be more engaged in what we were doing.

During the following winter, we worked on our covenant together for a few weeks, and Alyssa had become fully engaged in the process.[3] Ian wasn't present. He was very sporadic in his involvement because of his busy schedule of work and school. Alyssa, however, was becoming more and more involved, pushing into life on mission with our community.

As we worked on the covenant, we dealt with each rhythm in turn.

Eat

"If we lived like a family, how often do you think we'd eat together?" I asked. Some said every day; others said once a week.

"Keep in mind, we are also missionaries, sent by God to eat with others. It's not just about us," someone added.

This process revealed some unhealthy patterns in our group due to the busyness of life and the isolation in which many found themselves. Some rarely sat down to eat as a family in

---

[3] The formation of our missional community covenant didn't happen in just one night. It took several weeks. This is why I show us primarily working out rhythms in light of our identity as family, instead of going through each identity separately, as we normally do. This is not a verbatim account of what took place, but is meant to give you a feel for how this process can unfold. For a sample of what our completed covenant looked like, see Appendix B: Missional Community Covenant Sample, p. 241.

their own households, so eating regularly with others was a big challenge. We agreed that we needed to find a rhythm that would work in light of our present realities, while also pushing us to grow in caring for one another over a meal.

Adam recommended at least three meals a week: one where all of us would eat together, with each of us contributing to the meal (we eventually called this our family dinner); one where each of us would eat with some others during the week (this could be a coffee, a drink, or a night out as couples); and one where we would eat with some people who didn't yet know and believe the love of Jesus. We agreed on three meals out of our twenty-one meals a week. This seemed doable, yet it required all of us to rethink how our schedules reflected our love for one another.

Someone else added, "Let's continue to serve one another by providing meals during unique situations, like the first couple of weeks after one of us gives birth to a child." We also reminded one another that when summer arrived again, we would likely spend more time cooking out in the backyard and hanging around the fire pit together once more. This would be a great time to invite people not yet following Jesus to hang out with us. So we wrote that into our agreement as well.

Listen

"What about listening to God with one another and on behalf of one another? How should we go about that?" I asked.

"Let's make sure we make space to share our needs each week at our family dinner, then take time to pray together," Chelsey recommended. "I don't know if I really know how to effectively listen to God that well yet."

Adam shared, "What if we took some extended time together outside of the weekly meal to learn how to listen to God through his Word and prayer?"

"I think it's important that each of us grow in having some time alone with him to listen as well," Jayne chimed in.

Then I made a recommendation: "How about this? Let's take at least 15 to 20 minutes at our family gathering to share and pray at the end. And why don't some of us who want to learn how to listen to God better start meeting at least one morning a week together, and I will lead us in the practice of listening to God. Finally, can we all commit to having at least one extended time of prayer a week where we pray for the needs of others in the group and those we are reaching out to? Let's make sure we create some space to listen to God on behalf of others. What do you all think of that?"

They all agreed.

Then Nicki chimed in: "I can't do much, but I can pray. Please know that when any of you need prayer, I will pray. Just let me know."

"Why don't we create a group text message so we can quickly and easily inform one another when we need prayer?" I suggested. We all agreed, and set one up right on the spot.

Story

"Now, what about story?" I asked. "A good family truly knows one another and what makes us who we are today. Do you all know one another's stories?"

"Well, some of us who have been here longer know some of the stories," Matt said. "But there are some in the room here who don't know us well, and we don't really know their stories either. What if those of us who've been here longer each make it a point to have others who don't know our story over for dinner? Then, over dinner, we will share our stories with them. Then we will be eating, sharing our stories, and listening to one another. And those who are new to the family can share their stories with the whole group at our family meal. We could do one story a week for the next month or so."

"That's a great idea! Let's do that," the group responded.

"Let's not forget to go through *The Story of God*. Some of us here haven't gone through the whole story of the Bible. Can we do that soon?" Clay asked.

"That's a great suggestion," I said. "How about this? During the summer, we are likely going to meet more people who come to our cookouts. Many of them will not know the story of God's loving rescue through Jesus. Let's pray that some of them want to keep hanging out with us when it gets wet and dark around here again. If they do, let's ask if they want to go through *The Story* together in the fall." Everyone agreed.

"Hold on," one of our members said. "I love going through *The Story*, but I've never read through the entire Bible. Would any of you like to read through the whole Bible this year?" Not everyone in the group wanted to do this, but some did. Those who did agreed to help one another with this goal.

Throughout this time, Adam was playing the role of the scribe. He wrote all these ideas down.

Bless

"And blessing—remember, we have been blessed to be a blessing," I said. "How can we express that blessing toward one another? What has God given each of us? And do any of you have any needs that we can meet?"

"Well, some of you couples with kids need to be able to have a night out. What if I made myself available to watch your children?" Nikki asked.

Others shared how they wanted to be available to give financially if and when any of us were in need. Some offered up their skills of carpentry or housecleaning, and many other offers were made for how we would bless one another in the coming year. It was a great picture of God's family loving one another with whatever he had given us.

We also reminded one another that since our collective mission was the students, families, and teachers of Grant Elementary, as well as the neighborhood surrounding it, we would be blessing the school again this year through serving at the auction.

Celebrate

"OK, what about celebrating? How do we want to engage in this rhythm?" I asked. "I think we should celebrate every one of our birthdays."

"Yes, and anniversaries," someone said. "Think about how rare it is these days for people to stay married, especially in this region. Celebrating marriage and God's help in keeping us married is definitely what a family would do."

"Anything else?"

"Don't forget all the holidays. Let's watch the fireworks together on the Fourth of July and invite our friends to join us."

"And Halloween—that's how I came into this group in the first place. We should use that time of the year to invite more people into our community," Clay shared. "Let's do that together in the neighborhood."

"I'd love to do every holiday, but some of them, like Thanksgiving and Christmas, will be harder, as some of us are heading home to be with our biological families," another member said.

"Well, why don't we make sure no one is alone on those holidays then?" someone replied. "If anyone doesn't have a place to go, let's invite them to join us in one of our celebrations."

"Great! This all sounds good," I shared. "Is that everything?"

We were about to move on when someone said: "Wait a minute! We've got to keep celebrating Jesus together." I think we had all assumed that would happen. But we shouldn't have assumed.

"So, how are we going to keep him at the center of our celebrations?" I asked.

"Let's share Communion together every week," Adam suggested. "We can choose to go to the same gathering time on Sunday and take the meal together."

"That's good, but can we also take time at our weekly meal to pause and give time to express the ways God has blessed us, and then celebrate all the evidences of his grace in our lives?" someone suggested.

"Yes. Let's slow down and give thanks to him for his blessings regularly—as least weekly together at our meal."

ReCreate

"Now, how do we plan to recreate together?" I asked the group. "How should we keep the rhythm of resting, working, playing, creating, and restoring beauty in our lives apart and together?"

"Well, let's make sure we are all taking time off weekly to rest," someone said. "We could check in on one another in our DNA groups."

"Yes, I need that. I can tend to work and work and work, and never slow down to rest," I said.

"What about a monthly game night together?" someone suggested. "We could have a different home host it each time."

"Do we all have to come every time?" one person asked.

"No, of course not," I said. "But doing it regularly may help us get into a better rhythm of playing together."

"OK."

"I think we should get away at least once a year on a short vacation/retreat," Clay added.

"That's going to take some work," another chimed in.

"Well, I'll take responsibility for that," Clay responded. "In fact, let's go to Seabrook. That's the place where we first went away for the weekend with Jeff and Jayne. It could be like a reunion for us."

"This is great stuff, family!" Adam said as he continued to type.

Then Alyssa spoke up: "Throughout all of this, I have realized that I feel called to take care of the community garden in Nicki's backyard. It could be such a great blessing to so many people in this neighborhood. We could invite them to come take food whenever they need it. It would also be a great way for us to provide food for our family meals together. Besides, it's such a great picture of things being restored."

"I love it," I responded. I had been taking a lot of responsibility for the garden, and it was not being as well cared for as it needed to be. I also imagined how Alyssa's greater involvement in the family could be a big blessing to her, as well as bring Ian closer into our community.

"The only problem is, I don't really have the time to do it," Alyssa shared. "You see, Ian is in full-time school and working a part-time job, and I have a baby to take care of, while I'm also working a part-time job."

"Do you feel called to do this?" I asked.

"Yes, but I can't see how I could."

"Well, it's not your job to figure this out all by yourself," Matt said. "How can we help?"

"I don't have any idea how you can help," Alyssa responded.

"Well, what if you didn't have to work?" he asked.

"What are you talking about?" she exclaimed.

"Well, how much does your job provide? How much would you need if you quit your job?" he continued.

"What are you guys doing?" Alyssa asked hesitantly.

"We're family. This is what family does. We are here to help you do what God is calling you to do and support you to be able to do it," Matt went on. "So, how much would you need a month?"

"This is crazy!" Alyssa exclaimed.

"No, it's family," another stated.

"Really? You're serious? We would need $500," she said.

In about two minutes, the group committed to give $500 a month to Alyssa and Ian to free her up to be a stay-at-home mom who could serve the community and neighbors through caring for the garden.

"I can't take your money. I can't accept that," Alyssa exclaimed.

"Well, that's what a family does for one another," one of our group members reminded her.

"Have you already received what Jesus did for you?" Adam asked. "Did you accept the gift of God in sending his Son to die on the cross for your sins?"

"Yes," Alyssa replied.

"Well, then this is nothing. A gift of $500 a month is nothing compared to the life of God's only Son given for you. If you can receive him, you can receive this. His life is of infinitely greater value than this gift."

"Well, when you put it like that . . ."

"What other way is there?" another said.

"That is what the gospel leads us to do, Alyssa," I said. "We give because he gave to us. And we can receive because we've already received the most costly gift there is in Jesus."

"Well, I guess I can accept it then," she said.

Remember, the mission brings stuff to the surface, and the gospel is the answer to the question and the solution to the problem.

We found out later that only a few days prior, Alyssa had learned she was pregnant with their second child. She had asked

God to make it possible for her to be a stay-at-home mom. He had no problem answering her prayer.

That very night, she began posting on Facebook about what God had done to answer her prayer. Several of her friends who hadn't yet put their faith and trust in Jesus (as well as some who were Christians) questioned this act. "What's in it for them?" they asked. "There must be a catch. People don't just do this!" Alyssa had the opportunity to share the gospel and how what Jesus had done was leading our family to love her like we had been loved.

This love, and many other aspects of our life together, had a huge impact on Ian. Several months later, Ian decided to be baptized to express his faith in and submission to Jesus Christ. His father, Bill, and Bill's wife, Mee-zung, showed up for Ian's baptism. That fall, Bill and Mee-zung also joined our group and began going through *The Story* together. Five months later, Bill expressed his faith in Jesus through baptism. Just recently, Mee-zung did the same.

Our group supported Ian and Alyssa in this way throughout the rest of his education. Ian eventually graduated and received a job in his field in another state. They recently moved away, but for several years, they experienced the church as the family of God on mission together, serving others in tangible ways. I trust they will take what they learned and continue living it out in their new place.

The word and work of the gospel is spreading out, saturating every place, reaching all people through God's sent ones.

Where is he sending you? Across the street, across your city, across the country, or around the world? With whom do you believe you are being sent? How might you covenant together on this mission?

365

(17)

Everyday People
on Mission

The phone lit up: "Sondra, can I stop by?" It was a text message from a seventeen-year-old football player from Lincoln High School with whom Todd and Sondra had gotten acquainted. "Always!" she responded.

Todd and Sondra had made it clear that he could ask for help any time. Whatever he needed, whenever he needed it, they were available. They wanted him to see them as another family—another home—that he could come to at any time.

Todd and Sondra had been students in my very first youth ministry. They had learned to be disciples of Jesus who make disciples while they were in middle and high school. They also had been the first adults to join our core group when we started Soma seven years later. They had been a part of several missional communities by this point, and God had opened a new opportunity for them at Lincoln High School.

In a matter of minutes, the student was sitting at Sondra's table having a drink, while her three little boys ran about the house like Tasmanian devils, jumping on and off the couch. "How's work? School?" Sondra asked. "Are you getting prepared for college?" She cared for this teenager as if he were her own.

Then she asked, "How are things going for you living at your aunt's house?"

"I'm not there anymore," he said.

"What? Where are you living?"

"I have a new home."

"Really? Where?"

"Well, I found a couch to sleep on at a friend's place."

"Are you hungry?" Sondra asked. (What teenager isn't?)

"Yes." It turned out he hadn't eaten in days.

Sondra served up some leftovers, then dessert. He just kept eating. Then he brought his plate into the kitchen, where Sondra was cleaning up.

"How are you really doing?" she asked. "You seem a bit down."

He went on to share that he didn't have any food and he couldn't pay his cell phone bill. "I have some cash. I will give you what I have," Sondra said.

When she looked into her wallet, she saw a one-dollar bill and a hundred-dollar bill. She recalled God telling her, a few weeks earlier, to keep the hundred-dollar bill in her purse, just in case. The "just in case" moment was staring her in the face. God knew the student was going to need it, so he had directed Sondra to set it aside for him. Her resources were set aside for Jesus to use, and her heart was prepared for this kind of moment.

This story illustrates a key part of our ongoing discipleship—listening to and surrendering to God moment by moment, then being ready to serve others in light of how God has served us through Jesus. We should always be ready to be the means through which God blesses others.

We are the family of God who are servants of Jesus—his hands and feet to the world.

So Sondra handed the student the hundred-dollar bill. "That's all I've got," she stated.

"I can run and get change for you at 7–Eleven," he responded.

"No way! God told me weeks ago to keep it in my wallet, just in case someone was in need."

"Thank you!" he said while he gave Sondra a big hug. Then he went on his way.

A Meeting in the Basement

This ministry had begun prior to the previous football season, in the spring of 2013. I remember sitting with Todd and Sondra in a cinder-block office in the basement of Lincoln High School. It was the office of Jon Kitna, a former NFL quarterback, who had felt called to return to the high school he had attended to teach math and coach football. Actually, he was less concerned with math and football than with the hearts of the young men sitting under his teaching and training. Math and football were really just vehicles through which he could get to their hearts.

I had been meeting sporadically on Friday mornings with Jon and several other men to pray, study the Bible, and talk about how we could be the kind of men who might make a difference in our city. One time, Jon shared with me that a large percentage of the students at Lincoln had no dads present in their lives. I told him I thought we might have some people from Soma who would want to step into this vacuum with the presence and love of Jesus.

I thought of Todd and Sondra's missional community.

They had had previous seasons of fruitful ministry in their community, but they were wondering what was next. Their community was a very loving group of people. They knew how to love one another as a family. People were drawn to Todd and Sondra, and to the community they had created with Jesus's help. However, they knew it was not meant to end with them. They were called to be Jesus's servants and missionaries to a world that needs his help. They were part of his body, and this meant they needed to discover how he wanted to work through them to impact the world in a tangible way. They were wondering, "Where do you want us to go next as your missionaries, Lord?"

The answer turned out to be Lincoln High School—a place that needed an expression of God's kingdom to show up.

You need to ask similar questions about your life together with some others: "Where are you sending us together? And who do you want us to serve, Jesus? Who needs to see what your kingdom looks like? Who needs to feel the real touch of Jesus through our hands—through us? Who needs to hear of the Father's love for them available now through Jesus?"

Next, you need to ask: "What do they need? What aspects of Jesus's love in tangible form should we show them by how we serve? *How* can we show them what life is like in God's kingdom by the way we serve them?"

Such questions were on our minds as we met with Jon.

"Jon, how can we help? How can we serve you? What do the players need? How can we love them and serve them?" Todd asked. Jon went on to share story after story about boys who had so much potential but so little help: the boy who hadn't seen his dad since he was five, even though the man was only blocks away, selling drugs; the player who could have gotten a full scholarship to college if only he had filled out his application properly and on time; boys who practiced day after day and played their hearts out on Friday nights, with no one calling out their name from the stands. There were many young men without dads and without resources. These were lives in need of love, in need of help, in need of families. Our hearts were broken and gripped by the love of Christ for these boys! We knew something must be done to show them Christ's love.

Jon gave us a tour of the locker room and showed us where the girl team managers washed and folded practice and game jerseys. He pointed out some areas that needed repairs or painting: broken lockers and well-worn benches; chipped paint and flimsy shelves; disheveled equipment and poorly designed storage units. When we walked outside, Jon shared his dream about how the stadium and grounds could be restored. We saw more evidence of brokenness and plenty of opportunities for restoration to happen.

Jon talked, we walked—and a vision of loving restoration began to emerge. Clearly Jon had been thinking about this for a long time. We were catching his vision, and we could see that it was clearly part of Jesus's vision, too.

Sharing the Vision

Todd and Sondra began to share the vision with their missional community. At first, people struggled to understand how they could help. Some worked all day and came home late. How could they ever be with the players, since they practiced after school? Others were concerned about how they could serve, since they had little kids at home all day. Others were older and didn't have the energy level they once had. They were excited about the vision, but unable to see themselves playing any significant role.

I have found this to be the case so often. For some reason, our imaginations have been paralyzed. People have a hard time seeing outside of their present situations. So we have to help them.

That is why taking people through the missional community covenant process can be so helpful. How can a group of people from different walks and stages of life engage in everyday rhythms with these football players? Each of the six rhythms presented questions:

- Eat: Did the players need meals provided for them? Did they need companionship around a meal? What about having them over for dinner?
- Listen: How could we serve the players by listening to God on their behalf through prayer? How could we make time to be with them enough to ask questions and listen to their real needs?
- Story: Did we know the story of the place and people God was sending us to so that we would know how to serve them best? What had shaped Lincoln High School, and how might that story inform how we could care for the faculty and students?
- Bless: What did we have that they presently needed? How could we serve them with what we had?
- Celebrate: How could we engage in their celebrations? What kinds of celebrations did they have, and how might we serve at them? Did they have aspects of life that should be celebrated, but currently were not? How might we bring to the party the better wine and the servant towel?
- ReCreate: What did they enjoy doing that we could join in with? Where might we provide some rest in areas where they were overworked or overburdened? How could we engage in fun with them? What needed restoration, and how might we bring about beauty where there was brokenness?

Todd and Sondra knew they needed to lead their group of twenty-five adults and twenty kids to think more holistically.

"We can't think only about our weekly meeting," they said. "And we can't think about practice times or games alone. Let's think about the whole week. What can we do during the day, afternoons, evenings, and weekends? Let's think about their whole lives. How can all of us find a role in serving Lincoln football—not just the players, but the coaches, managers, and families as well? We all can be involved, but we have to think through the normal everyday stuff and not simply the event-based stuff. This isn't only about Friday night."

Just as my group had walked through the process of forming a covenant to reach out to our neighborhood and local elementary school, Todd and Sondra led their group toward the mission of Lincoln High School, starting with the football team. In partnership with Jon and Jeni Kitna, the group began to learn how they could best come alongside the team to love the players, serve them, and proclaim Jesus to them. It began with simply letting the Kitnas know that they could call Todd and Sondra whenever a need arose.

One of the first needs was a fund-raiser. The boys all needed to raise money for the football team, but few had contacts with people who could give. So the missional community hosted a fund-raising event at the Metronome, a local coffee shop owned by a member of Soma, who was doing business as mission. The group members invited everyone they knew who could give so they could hear the boys share their need. They asked them all to come prepared to give, or not to come. There was a great turnout, and the boys started to see that some people in the community actually cared about them.

Later, there was a need to provide rides for the boys, and the missional community showed up with a caravan (actually four minivans). Snacks were needed after practice. Volunteers were needed to serve at the football camp. Then, as football season began, the team needed women to work with the girl managers, washing jerseys, handing out towels, carrying equipment, and giving the players water. Others were needed to sell T-shirts at the games. And still others were called upon to sit in the stands and cheer for the players by name, ensuring that no boy was missed. Some in the group provided babysitting so that parents with little children were freed up to attend games or join the team on the bus for away games. Others gave financially when needs were made known, while some ran errands during the day with their kiddos in tow. All ages were involved in one way or another—everyone loving like family and serving as Jesus's body.

Intergenerational Service

Before the season began, Sondra thought of my parents. She recalled a key conversation I'd had with them while driving them to the Seattle-Tacoma airport after they had come to visit us for a couple of weeks. My dad had retired. As typical retired Michiganders, they spent their summers on the lake and their winters in Florida. There's nothing wrong with enjoying rest in the beauty of God's creation, and I would guess there are some people who engage these places intentionally for God's purposes, but this was not the case for my parents at that time. I was thinking about all that I had experienced growing up in our home. I had watched my parents love others so well, and I knew they still had much to give. I thought, "People still need to see the love of Jesus expressed through their lives today."

So there in my car, I told my dad: "You and Mom are so gifted by God. Mom, you have so much to give and so many things you could teach others about being a great wife and mother. And Dad, you have so many skills that young men need to learn. Do you know how many young men need to be trained by someone like you? You're both not done! Don't coast into heaven by spending the last years of your lives living for your-selves. I know the world tells you that you worked your whole life to retire, but Christians don't retire from Jesus's mission. You retire when you're dead! And you're not dead yet! These could be the best years of your lives! Do you know how many younger adults and parents would love to just sit at your feet and learn from your experiences? Are you aware of how many in this generation grew up with almost no parenting and no mentoring? You both are such an asset to Jesus and his work here! Jesus wants to keep working through you!"

Then I said: "So here's what I'm going to ask you to do. Take a month to ask God what he wants you to do with your lives. Ask him to direct you on how you are supposed to use your gifts and time. Pray about moving out here to Tacoma to join us. I want you to get busy making disciples and mentoring younger people in Muskegon, on the lake, in Florida, in another country, or with us here in Tacoma. Somewhere. What I'm not OK with is letting you waste the rest of your lives!"

My parents' eyes welled up with tears.

They knew God had more for them. God had designed them and saved them for so much more! The Spirit was tugging at their hearts.

You know it, too, if you have Jesus's Spirit in you.

If you belong to Jesus, his Spirit will do that in you. You are a new creation, so you have a new heart that wants to do what Jesus wants (Rom. 7:15–25). And his Spirit is in you, urging you to obey Jesus and join him on his mission.

As I dropped my parents off at the airport, I told them I would be calling them in a month to find out their answer.

Do you realize that the largest generation with the greatest amount of resources in the history of the United States is now in retirement: the baby boomers. And many of them are wasting their best years, living for themselves.

Is that you? Don't waste your retirement.

On the other hand, the members of the next largest generation, the millennials, are just growing up and entering some of the most significant places of influence in the world. But most of them have never been discipled by mentors who love Jesus.

Is this you? Don't make it all about you.

One generation is loaded with wisdom, time, and resources. The other has some of the greatest opportunities to change the world, but they need older mentors who love Jesus around them.

What are we going to do about that? Boomers, please give your life away to others! Finish well. Make it all about Jesus and his mission.

Millennials, you have many years ahead of you. Spend your years well and please ask for help! Ask an older disciple of Jesus to join you on your journey. Some of them don't know that you need it and that you want it. Don't go alone, like so many before you have done.

Why did I just go down this path? I did so because now is the time for us to get serious about Jesus's mission together, and we need all ages in this game. Church has to stop being about us. It's time for us to get back to what Jesus lived and died for. We need everyone in the game! If not, Jesus saturation will not happen.

Can you imagine what would happen if all those in retirement who know and love Jesus were to partner with the younger generation in this? Think about the thousands of missional communities that could be started all over the United States and around the world—and the thousands of people who would come to know and love Jesus as a result!

Stop and consider your life. How will you spend it, and for whom? Please take Jesus's call to make disciples seriously. What are you going to do with your life? It's never too late. Don't waste it.

I hope you're open to stepping out into what I believe Jesus is calling his church back to—Jesus communities on Jesus's mission, disciples who make disciples, together, not alone, in every place and in all of life.

Sondra is one of these younger leaders, and she knew that the mission to Lincoln High School could really use older, wiser people like my parents. She knew I had challenged my parents to consider joining our work in Tacoma. So she contacted them on Facebook to see if they would be willing to come back to Tacoma during football season to join their missional community in serving. My parents agreed! I couldn't believe it! They were going to join in the work of gospel saturation with Todd and Sondra at Lincoln High School—an older generation joining the younger one. I had been praying for something like this for a long time.

The football players loved my parents. They all looked up to my dad like a father, and my mom became the team mom—the girl managers especially loved her.

One of the pictures etched into my mind is my dad and one of the football players on their knees in the weight room.

One of the players had organized a chapel that took place in the weight room. A different missional community member was assigned each week to share a short gospel message. Then the boys were encouraged to break into groups with facilitators from the missional community to discuss the message while they ate pizza that a couple of moms from the group had picked up. One week, I was invited to share. Afterward, my dad had the privilege of leading one of the players to surrender his life to Jesus Christ. I didn't know it had happened until I looked over and saw them on their knees. My dad had tears streaming down his face as he joined this player in prayer. It was just like what I had so often seen my dad doing when I was a kid. My dad and mom were back in the game!

During one of the home games, another player suffered a head injury. He was a good student and a very talented football player. After he was taken off the field, he started to panic because he couldn't remember a thing from that day. Sondra and Emily, another member of the missional community, stopped and prayed for him right there on the field. The trainers checked him out and found he was OK.

More recently, this player needed to make some extra money, so he began selling stolen cell phones. He ended up making a transaction with a guy, but he decided to take the money, keep the phone, and run. The guy held one of the items and wouldn't let go, so this player beat the guy up badly and ended up in jail. While he was in jail, four of the coaches went to visit him. They asked, "Why didn't you come to us if you needed help?" He said he didn't know why. Later, he wrote a letter to Jon, telling him that he felt the need to be mentored and learn more about Jesus. Ryan, one of the men who are committed to this mission, now meets with him regularly.

Another player sent Sondra a text one day: "My dad was supposed to send me some money for prom, but just texted and said he can't now." She then sent out a text to the missional community, and they quickly collected cash for him. This situation eventually led to a conversation with this player about budgeting. The group asked him if they could help him make a plan before he headed to college. He agreed that he needed their help.

Going to games, helping at practices, washing jerseys, handing out water, praying for injuries, bringing pizza, training on budgeting, tutoring students, babysitting so others can serve, giving money when needed—the opportunities are endless.

The family of God sent as missionary servants to the Lincoln High School football team is made up of all ages. And all of them are part of making disciples who make disciples there.

Small, Everyday Acts

Todd and Sondra's missional community continued to love, serve, and care for the team. And the chapels continued week after week. The season was coming to an end, so Jon Kitna spoke at the last chapel. After he finished, he invited the boys to respond to Jesus's call to surrender their lives to him. Eight boys bowed their knees to Jesus that day!

They felt loved like family. They were served by Jesus's body. The message was proclaimed. And they believed.

Sondra recently shared with me: "Before we started serving our local high school last year, I had just watched the movie *The Hobbit: An Unexpected Journey*, and the line that stuck out to me was this one by Gandalf the wizard: 'I have found it is the small, everyday deeds of ordinary folk that keep the darkness at bay. Small acts of kindness and love.'"

Too often, we focus on the spectacular activities of a few prominent Christians, leaving many people feeling as if what they do in everyday life doesn't really matter. But the everyday stuff, done with gospel intentionality in the name of Jesus, changes lives as well.

I have found that when we love and serve people like Jesus loved and served us, it gives great evidence to how powerful the gospel is to change lives. Then, when we proclaim what Jesus did in serving us, people who hear also see Jesus serving them through his body—through us, his church.

They see normal people on Jesus's mission getting to experience extraordinary life together!

The story of this missional community living lives on mission as Jesus's servants to Lincoln High School continues. Recently, while visiting some students at the school, Sondra and Ryan met a girlfriend of one of the football players. They discovered that she, her little brother, and her dad were homeless. She asked them if they might have a duffle bag she could use to transport her clothes whenever they had to move. Sondra picked up a pink duffle bag for her. A few weeks later, she ran into the same girl in the hallway at the school and connected her to Greg, who directs our transitional housing for homeless families (the same Greg from chapter 2).

Greg and Mary's decision to come to a poker party with Jesus's people on mission in the everyday stuff of life led to a family coming to faith, a marriage being restored, and a ministry to homeless families in our city.

A high school youth group in Seattle that called and trained students to make disciples in everyday life led to Todd and Sondra's becoming disciple-makers of their peers and eventually of a football team.

A direct word to a couple in retirement, followed by a call from a family (Todd and Sondra) on mission, led to my parents getting back into the game and leading some high school boys to Jesus.

More recently, I received this note from Sondra:

> Ryan and I had a meeting with the principal. We wanted to get a broader idea of how we can care for the school as a whole. After talking with him and another teacher, we decided to put together a resource list of people and skills we have in our missional community in order to help the staff direct kids to us for extra help and encouragement. They also suggested that we have some people available to help with tangible, daily needs of the kids. For example: if a student gets suspended and they can't get in touch with the parents/guardians, they would call one of us to come pick up the student and take them out to lunch to build a relationship and care for the kid. When they suggested this, I almost jumped out of my seat, saying: "Yes, that's exactly what we want to do! We want to care for the kids' hearts." Following this meeting, we decided to have a breakfast at the school with our missional community, the principal,

and some teachers. We had another Soma family watch our kids at one of our homes so that all of us were freed up to be at the breakfast. The breakfast was awesome! They and Jon Kitna all shared what they need help with as a staff, as well as what the students need. The opportunities are endless! This mission is way bigger than us. But it's just another opportunity for God to do *big* things through normal people!

Not long ago, Soma lost its usage of the building where we met on Sundays. We were without a meeting place for more than a year. Some local churches were very gracious to allow us to use their facilities when they didn't need them, but we desperately wanted to get back to meeting on Sunday mornings. As a result of Todd and Sondra's missional community serving Lincoln High School, the principal asked Soma to start gathering in the school auditorium. He wants more of Soma at Lincoln High School! And in the past couple of weeks, we have had the privilege of baptizing some of the students in the Lincoln High School pool!

What started as a meeting with a couple of people in a cinder-block office in the basement of Lincoln High School led to a missional community getting the joy of seeing some football players' lives changed by the gospel. And now we have the privilege of serving an entire school as the hands and feet of Jesus in Tacoma.

Who knows what is still in store as Jesus works through his people to bring about gospel saturation in Tacoma through his family of missionary servants in this part of our city? There are more chapters to come, I'm sure.

And there are many more chapters that God plans to write through you.

What part will you play in the story he is writing? Whom is he sending you to love, serve, and proclaim Jesus to? Who will you do it with?

He plans to saturate the earth with his glory through us, his church, making disciples of Jesus in the everyday stuff of life.

Don't be a spectator. Get in the game and watch him do great things through you!

Conclusion

The Seeds of a Movement

It has taken far too long for me to write this conclusion. I tried over and over again to write it, but I was never satisfied. I was stuck and I didn't know why.

Then, the other day, it hit me. I don't want to end this because I don't want this to end.

Well, I want the writing of the book to end—really, I do! It's been harder than I thought. And I want you to finish this book; thanks for making it this far!

What I don't want to end are the chapters that still need to be written—by you!

At the beginning of this book, I stated that I wrote it not because I've always wanted to write a book, but because I want to see our world saturated with the good news of Jesus everywhere.

I've had a hard time writing a conclusion because I don't want *you* to conclude. I don't want *you* to come to an end. I don't want *you* to close this book and go back to life as normal. I want you to live a new life in light of Jesus, your new identity, and the mission he has saved you for and sent you on.

I realized that I want you to have your moment in the boat with Jesus, just like I did. I want you to hear him call you to begin something with him. But I know that there is nothing I can write that will make that happen. I can't make you sit in that boat with Jesus and walk out on the water toward what he is calling you to do.

So I didn't know what to write.

Then he showed me again that just as I needed that time with him in the boat, so do you. He also showed me again that this is not about me, not about how well I write a book. Neither is it about how well you read and apply it. It is about his work in you in your own boat. He has you where he wants you and he plans to lead you forward.

And yet, he also reminded me that he can plant seeds through the words in this book, and those seeds can produce in you the faith that can enable you both to hear Jesus's call in the boat and lead you toward Jesus's mission when you step out of the boat.

I do some gardening. I'm not a great gardener, but I enjoy it nonetheless. Sometimes I think I enjoy it because, in this work of making disciples, I often don't see immediate fruit from my labors, but when I'm gardening, I do. When I plant seeds, I get plants. Eventually, those plants grow and produce juicy, red raspberries, ripe, luscious tomatoes, and sweet, crispy green cucumbers. I till the soil, plant the seeds, water the ground, hope and pray for plenty of sunshine in our rain-rich, cloudy Northwestern climate, and trust that the seeds will do what seeds do. And every year, I get a harvest that satisfies the longings of my children's tastebuds and fills the bellies of our missional community and neighbors.

Also, every year we have more fruit than we can pick or eat, and inevitably some falls to the ground and decomposes. When it does, the seeds get replanted. The following year, plants grow that I did not personally plant. Gardeners call these plants "volunteers." They voluntarily grow without our help. I do nothing to make them come about except plant the initial seeds. The plants and the soil do the rest.

Unfortunately, the weeds in my garden do the same thing. They drop their seeds. And every year, I have to pull out weeds where I pulled weeds the previous year.

Seeds fall to the ground. Plants spring up. More seeds are created. And the process continues. This is God's design, not just with plants, but with everything, including you and me.

Throughout this book, I have been planting seeds. I hope they are gospel seeds and not the seeds that produce the weeds of the flesh and the world.

Paul tells the Galatians, "Do not be deceived: God is not mocked, for whatever one sows, that will he also reap" (Gal. 6:7).

We are all planting seeds all of the time.

In fact, I've come to realize that we are also making disciples all of the time. In every moment when we are with others, we are planting seeds of what we believe in and leading people to follow us in what we believe life should be like.

The question isn't, "Are we sowing?" We are sowing seeds all of the time.

And the question isn't, "Are we making disciples?" We are always making disciples.

People are watching, learning, and listening to what we believe and how we live, and we are discipling them toward someone or something.

Paul goes on to say, "For the one who sows to his own flesh will from the flesh reap corruption, but the one who sows to the Spirit will from the Spirit reap eternal life" (v. 8).

I hope that the seeds I sowed throughout this book were sown to the Spirit, because what I want for you is eternal life. Eternal life is not "life after death" only. Eternal life is life abundant (John 10:10), life in close relationship with God (John 17:3), life that you can have with him right now in this world.

However, this isn't just about what I wrote or how I wrote it. This is about what Jesus wants to plant in you and what you do with it.

I trust that he has been planting seeds all along as you've been reading. Now you can sow to the flesh or the Spirit. You can walk away from this book and live like you've always lived. You can also try to put into practice some of what I have written here, but do it in your own strength or for your own glory. Both would be sowing to the flesh. If you do either, it will choke out the life in you and in others as well, leading to more brokenness and destruction.

Or you could sow seeds and make disciples. Jesus wants you to sow to the Spirit and experience eternal life. And he wants you to make disciples who will also experience eternal life.

My prayer is that you will sow to the Spirit. My hope is that you will seek Jesus's glory in all of this and will depend not on your own strength but on His Spirit. If you do, you will be like the vegetable plants in my garden. You will drop seeds wherever you go: gospel seeds in your home, at work, at the café, and along the path everywhere you walk. Those seeds you sow will, by the Spirit, produce more life and fruit, leading to more seeds sown.

That kind of seed sowing leads to a movement from one life to the next to the ends of the earth. That's how God designed it to work.

It won't end with this book. It won't end with you. This doesn't have to end.

Your life was meant to be a seed-sowing life leading to a life-changing movement of Jesus saturation to the ends of the earth.

But it has to begin in a boat, the boat he's got you in today, and the seeds he is sowing in your heart must lead to a step out of the boat. Each step you take in the Spirit will lead to seed-sowing ripples that could change the world.

He did it in Peter. He's doing it in me. He's doing it in Greg and Mary, Todd and Sondra, Randy and Lisa, Ian and Alyssa, my mom and dad, and many, many more.

Now he wants to do it through you.

Surrender to Jesus.

Devote yourself to his mission.

Remember and live in light of your new identity.

Get on mission with a small group of people.

Covenant together to sow seeds to others in the everyday rhythms of life, and watch the movement ripple out of your life until the whole earth is saturated with the good news of Jesus.

This isn't a conclusion—this is your commission!

Appendix A

Missional Community Covenant Template

This template serves as a guide for a committed group of Christians to form a plan together for being Jesus's disciples on mission. You may want to preface the forming of this covenant by doing a study on the gospel, your new identity in Christ, and the mission of making disciples. Or you could form your covenant while doing a study on each of those important topics.

Gospel

I believe the gospel is the power of God for salvation through faith in the person and work of Jesus Christ saving me for the purpose of glorifying God and participating in his mission of saturation through making disciples who make disciples.

I believe I *have been saved* from the penalty of sin . . .

- I believe I was an enemy of God because of my sin and rebellion against him, deserving his wrath.
- I believe Jesus is the Son of God who is fully God and fully man and that he lived his life fully submitted to God the Father.
- I believe Jesus died on the cross for my sins according to the Scriptures.
- I believe Jesus rose again on the third day and appeared to many people.

- I believe Jesus ascended to the right hand of the Father and sent his Spirit to convict the world of sin, righteousness, and judgment.
- I believe the Holy Spirit has made me alive in Christ and I am now no longer condemned, but a new creation, loved by God as Father, submitted to Jesus as Lord, and sent and empowered by the Spirit for the mission of making disciples.

I believe I *am being saved* from the power of sin . . .

- I believe that the Holy Spirit who raised Jesus from the dead now lives in me and I have access to the power of God to overcome sin and Satan today.
- I believe it is God's will that I be sanctified—set apart to do his will.
- I desire to obey God and continue to grow in becoming more like Jesus and accomplishing his mission.
- I believe I have all I need to make this a reality—his Spirit, his Word, and his church—and I intend to steward all of this for his glory.

I believe I *will be saved* from the presence of sin . . .

- I believe Jesus will one day return and will make an end to sin, suffering, evil, and brokenness.
- I believe there will be a new heaven and a new earth.
- I believe he will judge the living and the dead, and all those who put their trust in Jesus's life, death, and resurrection on their behalf will enjoy being in God's presence forever in the new heaven and new earth.
- I believe all those who trust in something or someone other than Jesus for their life and justification before God will be separated from God forever.
- I believe it is our job as the church to proclaim the gospel of Jesus Christ for the salvation of souls and to display

through our lives a foretaste of the future so that people will hunger for it and put their faith in Jesus Christ.

Gospel Identity

I believe that I have been given a new identity in Christ. I am now a child of God (family) sent by the power of the Spirit (missionary) to serve our King (servant) in fulfilling his mission to be disciples who make disciples.

Missionaries

We are Holy Spirit-filled missionaries sent as disciples to make disciples.

How will we commit ourselves as disciples who make disciples in the power of the Spirit?

1. Which people group will be our missional focus?
2. In what places should we regularly hang out in order to build relationships with those we want to reach?
3. How will we invite others to join us at the table? How often will we try to eat with others we are trying to reach?
4. How will we commit to listening prayer for those God is sending us to?
5. What specifically will we do so that the people to whom we are sent will hear the gospel this year (i.e., go through *The Story of God*, share our story with them, engage in a study, etc.)?
6. How will we engage in celebrating with the people group God is sending us to?
7. What celebrations are missing, where can we bring the better wine, or where can we bring the servant towel to the party?
8. How will we bless those we are being sent to in word or deed?

9. How will we play and rest with those God is sending us to?

10. What steps should each of us take this year to grow as disciples who make disciples (help each person identify at least two to three goals)?

Servants

We are servants of King Jesus committed to serving others.

How will we tangibly demonstrate the impact of the gospel in service to King Jesus?

1. What would good news look like to the people group we are sent to?

2. What needs beautifying in our missional focus?

3. How might we demonstrate Jesus's rule and reign through tangible service to those God is sending us to?

4. What specific projects or events do we need to accomplish or get involved in to demonstrate the restorative work of the kingdom of God?

5. How will we serve the disconnected or underresourced among the people we are sent to?

6. How can we encourage one another to see our vocations and jobs as worship to our King?

7. How could we serve together during our weekly celebrations with the larger body?

8. How will we walk through Spirit-led giving to the church and others?

9. How can we commit to help one another grow in serving in light of their unique design by God (i.e., identify spiritual gifts or personality types; write out personal mission statements; etc.)?

10. How will we intentionally share what we have with one another and those in need?

Family

We are children of God who love one another as family.

How will we express our love as brothers and sisters adopted by the Father?

1. How will we commit to listening prayer for one another?
2. What study or training do we need to go through as a group in light of where we all need to grow (keep in mind personal discipleship goals)?
3. What actions will we commit to in order to express our love for one another as brothers and sisters (think of the one-another passages)?
4. Are any of us who believe the gospel not yet baptized? What next steps should we take in obeying Jesus's command to be baptized (Matt. 28:19–20)?
5. How will we honor the leaders in the larger church family appointed to shepherd us?
6. How will we make sure all of us know one another's stories?
7. How will we celebrate Communion together?
8. What meals will we share with one another, and how often?
9. In what ways will we intentionally celebrate together, and around what?
10. What regular rhythms of recreating will we commit to together?

I, _____ , commit, with God's help, from
NAME

_____ to _____ , to live in light of my new identity in Christ
START DATE   END DATE

in these ways with my missional community.

_____   _____
SIGNATURE   DATE

Appendix B

Missional Community Covenant Sample

Below is an example of a missional community covenant agreed to by the Wedge Missional Community. This community includes approximately twelve adults and ten children. The group is primarily focused on serving the families, students, faculty, and neighborhoods around Grant Elementary School.

Gospel

I believe the gospel is the power of God for salvation through faith in the person and work of Jesus Christ saving me for the purpose of glorifying God and participating in his mission of saturation through making disciples who make disciples.

I believe I *have been saved* from the penalty of sin . . .

- I believe I was an enemy of God because of my sin and rebellion against him, deserving his wrath.
- I believe Jesus is the Son of God who is fully God and fully man and that he lived his life fully submitted to God the Father.
- I believe Jesus died on the cross for my sins according to the Scriptures.
- I believe Jesus rose again on the third day and appeared to many people.

- I believe Jesus ascended to the right hand of the Father and sent his Spirit to convict the world of sin, righteousness, and judgment.
- I believe the Holy Spirit has made me alive in Christ and I am now no longer condemned, but a new creation, loved by God as Father, submitted to Jesus as Lord, and sent and empowered by the Spirit for the mission of making disciples.

I believe I *am being saved* from the power of sin . . .

- I believe that the Holy Spirit who raised Jesus from the dead now lives in me and I have access to the power of God to overcome sin and Satan today.
- I believe it is God's will that I be sanctified—set apart to do his will.
- I desire to obey God and continue to grow in becoming more like Jesus and accomplishing his mission.
- I believe I have all I need to make this a reality—his Spirit, his Word, and his church—and I intend to steward all of this for his glory.

I believe I *will be saved* from the presence of sin . . .

- I believe Jesus will one day return and will make an end to sin, suffering, evil, and brokenness.
- I believe there will be a new heaven and a new earth.
- I believe he will judge the living and the dead, and all those who put their trust in Jesus's life, death, and resurrection on their behalf will enjoy being in God's presence forever in the new heaven and new earth.
- I believe all those who trust in something or someone other than Jesus for their life and justification before God will be separated from God forever.
- I believe it is our job as the church to proclaim the gospel of Jesus Christ for the salvation of souls and to display

through our lives a foretaste of the future so that people will hunger for it and put their faith in Jesus Christ.

Gospel Identity

I believe that I have been given a new identity in Christ. I am now a child of God (family) sent by the power of the Spirit (missionary) to serve our King (servant) in fulfilling his mission to be disciples who make disciples.

Missionaries

We are Holy Spirit-filled missionaries sent as disciples to make disciples.

How will we commit ourselves as disciples who make disciples in the power of the Spirit?

1. We believe we are sent to the faculty, students, family, and surrounding area of Grant Elementary School.
2. We also plan to support "making disciples of all nations" by supporting Yoshito Noguchi planting a church in Tokyo.
3. We will regularly engage in monthly school activities (school dances, parties, game nights, etc.).
4. We will frequent restaurants and cafés on 6th Avenue.
5. Some of the women will join the indoor women's soccer team that plays on Thursday nights.
6. Some will coach or be involved with kids through soccer or football.
7. We all will try to have one weekly intentional engagement over a meal, a drink, or an activity with people in this context.
8. We will provide weekly campfire/s'mores nights during the summer to invite friends to.
9. We will serve at the Friday night cookouts on the Grant campus in June and July.

10. We will go through *The Story-Formed Way*[1] together in the fall with new friends.

11. We will set aside time to pray together for those in need in the community—minimally at our weekly family meal.

12. Each missional community member will go through the personal discipleship assessment tool and work with others in the group to identify two to three action plans for development.

Servants

We are servants of King Jesus committed to serving others.

How will we tangibly demonstrate the impact of the gospel in service to King Jesus?

1. We will serve at the yearly auction to raise money for arts education and the funding of special school events. This will include hosting planning meetings, serving on the planning team, and executing the actual auction.

2. Some of us will participate in the weekend backpack program to ensure students go home with food for the weekend.

3. Some of the moms will be teacher's assistants in the school.

4. We will financially give toward special needs that arise.

5. We will prepare and plant the community garden and care for it throughout the season, then share the harvest with the neighborhood and community.

6. We will restore Nicki's home for Jonathan to move into and eventually provide another missional community meeting place.

7. We will help one another in DNA groups to grow in worshiping Jesus through our daily jobs.

---

[1] To learn more about *The Story-Formed Way* curriculum, please visit www.saturatetheworld .com/the-story-formed-way

8. We will provide child care for people to have date nights and go away on weekend getaways.

9. We will ensure that each of us has a well-thought-out budget with generous giving to the church and community in place.

10. We will all share in providing for our weekly meal.

Family

We are children of God who love one another as family.

How will we express our love as brothers and sisters adopted by the Father?

1. We will share a weekly meal together that we all contribute to.

2. We will ensure we are all part of a DNA group that is studying the Bible together and helping one another grow in repentance, faith, and obedience to God's Word.

3. We will make time weekly to pray for one another.

4. Some of us will commit to read through the Bible in a year.

5. We will commit to put away all falsehood and speak truthfully to one another, not putting up with gossip or slander.

6. We will commit to connecting with one another outside of planned weekly events through social media and special outings together.

7. Some will take responsibility to ensure a monthly game night occurs.

8. We will attend the weekly gathering with the larger body and take Communion together.

9. We will make sure we all know one another's stories. When a new person joins, we will hear his or her story and then invite him or her over for dinner to hear each of ours over the course of a few months.

10. We will go away once a year on a weekend retreat together.

11. We will celebrate one another's birthdays and throw baby showers for new mothers to be.

I,   <u>Jeffrey T. Vanderstelt</u> , commit, with God's help, from
NAME

<u>1/31/14</u> to <u>12/31/14</u>, to live in light of my new identity in Christ
START DATE   END DATE

in these ways with my missional community.

<u>   *Jeffrey T. Vanderstelt*   </u>   <u> *Dec. 31, 2013* </u>
SIGNATURE   DATE

General Index

Scripture Index